Vintage Details

A Fashion Sourcebook

Vintage Details
A Fashion Sourcebook

Jeffrey Mayer & Basia Szkutnicka
Photography by Stephen Sartori

Laurence King Publishing

Published in 2016 by
Laurence King Publishing Ltd
361–373 City Road
London EC1V 1LR
e-mail: enquiries@laurenceking.com
www.laurenceking.com

Reprinted 2019

A catalogue record for this book is
available from the British Library.

ISBN: 978 1 78067 742 2

Printed in China

Laurence King Publishing is
committed to ethical and sustainable
production. We are proud
participants in The Book Chain
Project®
bookchainproject.com

Cover: Greige wool crepe sleeveless
mini-cocktail dress, USA, ca.1968,
by Donald Brooks. Photographed by
Stephen Sartori.

Contents

Introduction

The work of directional fashion designers is well represented within the world's famous historic-garment repositories; we are familiar with designers such as Charles Frederick Worth, Paul Poiret, Gabrielle 'Coco' Chanel, Christian Dior and Yves Saint Laurent as influential arbiters of style. Not so familiar are the lesser-known names and brands, as well as the home dressmakers, who have also produced valid, creative and, at times, groundbreaking work.

Vintage Details unlocks the treasures of a little-known fashion collection, whose contents – garments from lesser-known designers and brands – might otherwise remain unseen and eventually be forgotten, and presents stunning, carefully selected details from these clothes. The intention of the authors is to provide inspiration to new generations of designers.

The Syracuse University's historic clothing collection, of which Jeffrey Mayer is curator, was established in the 1930s and gained a major benefactor in the early 1980s in alumnus Leon M. Genet, who contributed to and built support for the collection. It is now known as the Sue Ann Genet Costume Collection and Research Center in memory of his first wife, a talented textile artist and sculptor who drew inspiration from color, texture and fiber arts. This collection consists of approximately 2,500 women's garments and accessories dating from 1820 to the present day and is housed within the Fashion Design Department in the School of Design, part of the College of Visual and Performing Arts at Syracuse University, New York.

Both fashion designers originally, now academics, Jeffrey Mayer and Basia Szkutnicka have collaborated to document fashion details from both the Sue Ann Genet Costume Collection and from Szkutnicka's extraordinary private collection, selecting garments that make explicit style statements. This book records never-before-seen fashion information as a source of inspiration for designers, students and dressmakers.

The selection and subsequent editing of all the styles to be included in this book was an enormous project, and recording the garments themselves required the skill of a talented and sensitive photographer. Stephen Sartori spent hours learning about the intricacies of clothes in order to help reveal the construction secrets of little-known designers.

Jeffrey Mayer graduated from the University of Connecticut with an advanced degree in Fashion History. In 1992 he was appointed to Syracuse University, New York, where he teaches History of Dress, as well as designing womenswear, with partner Todd Conover, for their own label Conover Mayer.

'For me, the fascination with historic clothing is that remnants of the past – really personal items – were carefully saved and preserved. Unlike furniture or other decorative items, clothing is the most personal of all objects: items that were made by or exclusively chosen by someone to represent their personality to the world. These garments communicated the wearer's interests, beliefs, ideals and place in society, as well as giving the wearer the knowledge that, intrinsically, these garments would somehow transform their physical appearance. Working with historic clothing gives me the ability to connect with designers whom I will never meet, during a time when they were answering their own set of design questions. Their creativity and ingenuity, like their DNA, remains in their work.'

Basia Szkutnicka graduated from Central St Martins School of Art, London, in womenswear in the late 1980s and has designed for her own label, as well as working as a freelance design consultant and visiting lecturer at fashion schools worldwide. She is based at the London College of Fashion in the role of Study Abroad Director and Design lecturer. She discovered vintage clothing at the age of 14.

'Cast as Shylock in a school production of Shakespeare's *The Merchant of Venice*, I had to create my own costume. In a room of dressing-up clothes used for drama, above the school chapel, I found three gems: a pale-green, hand-embroidered, drop-waisted silk dress; a glass-beaded black belt with clattering tassels; and a length of luscious black cloth. The dress was early 1920s, the belt mid-Victorian and the cloth an extraordinary silk-velvet devoré. Discreetly, the precious items found their way into my school bag and then home. I still have the dress – it was my first ever vintage garment.

That's how the obsession began. Brought up with the polyester, throwaway clothes of the 1970s, I found old garments salvaged from jumble sales, charity shops and car boot sales so much more special. Their very fabric contained the past and, with this added ingredient, they were things to be preserved and loved. Vintage clothes are externally seductive and internally informative, and it is their construction as well as their embellishments that have always drawn me to collect and wear them.

Many years and many garments, shoes and bags later, the time has come to share my adoration with others.'

Visual Index

The index that follows features every piece of clothing being showcased in this book. It gives a front and back view of the garment, a description with suggested date, and a list of the pages on which the details can be found. The chapter titles have been abbreviated as follows:

Necklines **NLI**
Collars **CLR**
Sleeves **SLV**
Cuffs **CUF**
Pockets **PKT**
Fastenings & Buttonholes **F/BU**
Hems, Darts, Stitching & Fitting Devices **H/D/S/FD**
Pleats, Frills & Flounces **P/F/F**
Embellishment **EMB**
Surface **SFC**
Construction **CON**

Ivory silk sleeveless
sheath dress with
lace flounced skirt,
USA, ca.1924

Black silk coat
with ermine trim,
USA, ca.1925

Black satin dress with
handmade lace inset
at front, USA, ca.1925

Rose-pink chiffon
long-sleeved knee-
length dress with
cream lace inset
at front, sleeves and
hem, USA, ca.1925

Purple devoré coat,
USA, ca.1926

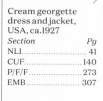

Cream georgette
dress and jacket,
USA, ca.1927

Fuchsia silk georgette day dress embellished with horizontal, pleated ruffles, USA, ca.1930

Black wool crepe day dress with black devoré sleeves and collar, USA, ca.1932

Blue, yellow and red paisley-print cotton voile day dress with drawstring pockets, USA, ca.1932

Yellow and red printed cotton bell-bottomed pants, USA, ca.1932

Floral-print chiffon dress with ruffles at neckline and hem, USA, ca.1935

Black synthetic crepe evening dress embellished with silk flowers and beaded wheat motif, USA, ca.1935

Black silk velvet and
cream lace evening
dress, USA, ca.1935

Purple velvet floor-
length evening dress,
USA, ca.1935

Green chenille
knitted dress with
¾-length skirt and
sleeves, USA, ca.1935

White cotton eyelet-
embroidered dress
with cape collar,
USA, ca.1935

Black and white
polka-dot silk
charmeuse evening
dress, USA, ca.1935

Black crepe dress
with circular ruffled
sleeves lined in white
faille, USA, ca.1935

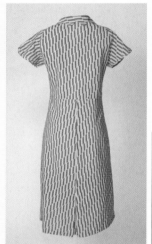

Red silk shantung
drd with matching
bolero, USA, ca.1960

Section	Pg
PKT	168
F/BU	209
EMB	329

Green, red, yellow and
blue printed cotton
full-skirted dress,
USA, ca.1960

Section	Pg
P/F/F	286
SFC	359

Navy-blue and
white silk novelty-
weave skirt suit,
USA, ca.1960

Section	Pg
CLR	89
PKT	168
H/D/S/FD	249

Oatmeal-colored
wool short-sleeved
day dress with
separate back panel,
France(?), ca.1962

Section	Pg
F/BU	211
H/D/S/FD	250

Bronze-colored
shantung skirt suit
with ¾-length sleeves,
USA, ca.1962

Section	Pg
NLI	50
H/D/S/FD	250
EMB	329

Red wool double-
breasted day suit,
USA, ca.1962

Section	Pg
CLR	91
CUF	149

VINTAGE DETAILS

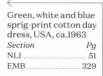

Green, white and blue
sprig-print cotton day
dress, USA, ca.1963
Section   *Pg*
NLI..........................51
EMB.....................329

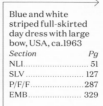

Blue and white
striped full-skirted
day dress with large
bow, USA, ca.1963
Section   *Pg*
NLI..........................51
SLV 127
P/F/F.....................287
EMB.....................329

Gray wool sheath
dress embroidered
with pussy willow,
USA, ca.1963
Section   *Pg*
NLI..........................50
H/D/S/FD...............252
EMB.....................331
SFC 360

Pink and white
patterned scoop-
necked dress with
matching short
jacket, USA, ca.1965
Section   *Pg*
CLR.........................91
F/BU......................212
EMB.....................331

Black synthetic crepe
sheath dress with
full-length organza
lantern sleeves,
USA, ca.1965
Section   *Pg*
SLV 128
CUF.........................151
H/D/S/FD...............257

Yellow silk faille
evening dress,
USA, ca.1965
Section   *Pg*
NLI..........................53
F/BU......................215
P/F/F.....................288
EMB.....................333
CON......................385

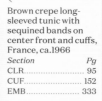

Brown crepe long-sleeved tunic with sequined bands on center front and cuffs, France, ca.1966

Pink, blue and yellow wool tweed short-sleeved sheath dress, USA, ca.1966

Cream silk satin sheath dress with padded hem, USA, ca.1966

Cream wool sheath dress embellished with silver-sequin polka-dots, France, ca.1966

Black crepe sheath dress, USA, ca.1967

Bottle-green zibeline cocktail dress, USA, ca.1967

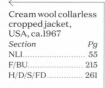

Cream silk tunic with beaded bib and cuffs, USA, ca.1968

Cream heavy wool coat dress, USA, ca.1968

Gray wool long-sleeved dress with pink velvet bow and cream satin collar and cuffs, USA, ca.1968

Orange Art-Deco-print chiffon long-sleeved sheath dress, USA, ca.1968

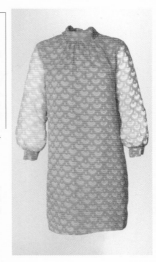 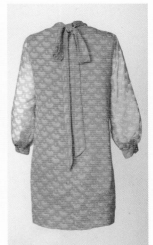

Black asymmetrical wool jacket with single-button closure, USA, ca.1968

Black silk faille ¾-length jacket, USA, ca.1968

Black velvet jumpsuit with appliquéd organdie sleeves and hem, USA, ca.1969

Ivory antique satin floor-length A-line dress, USA, ca.1969

Navy-blue and cream wool double-knit short-sleeved sheath dress, Italy, ca.1969

White seersucker long-sleeved minidress, USA, ca.1969

Taupe sleeveless sheath dress with matching long-sleeved coat, USA, ca.1969

Black, red, pink, blue and yellow wool long-sleeved ankle-length turtleneck dress with embroidered detailing, USA, ca.1969

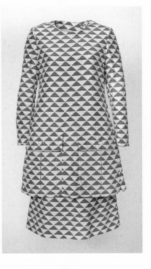

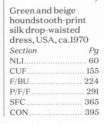

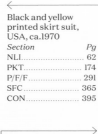

Cream wool double-knit long-sleeved day dress with brown synthetic leather piping, USA, ca.1983

Turquoise silk charmeuse batwing dress, China, ca.1985

Cream wool challis bodice with long sleeves and circular peplum, USA, ca.1985

Black wool waist-length jacket, USA, ca.1994

Black silk satin ruffle-pocket jacket, USA, ca.1995

Black silk satin jacket with clover-leaf neckline, USA, ca.1995

Necklines

Cream silk short-
sleeved day dress with
cream lace overskirt,
USA, ca.1920
(p.10)

Black velvet *robe de
style* with jagged hem
and poppy trim,
USA, ca.1924
(p.11)

Robin's-egg-blue silk
taffeta sleeveless *robe
de style*, USA, ca.1924
(p.11)

Rose-pink chiffon long-sleeved knee-length dress with cream lace inset at front, sleeves and hem, USA, ca.1925 (p.12)

Black satin dress with handmade lace inset at front, USA, ca.1925 (p.12)

Cream georgette dress and jacket, USA, ca.1927 (p.12)

Floral-print chiffon dress with ruffles at neckline and hem, USA, ca.1935 (p.14)

VINTAGE DETAILS

Green chenille knitted dress with ¾-length skirt and sleeves, USA, ca.1935 (p.15)

White, green, yellow, red and violet bamboo-print silk crepe evening dress, USA, ca.1935 (p.16)

Black silk velvet and cream lace evening dress, USA, ca.1935 (p.15)

Back view of left dress

Black and white polka-dot silk charmeuse evening dress, USA, ca.1935 (p.15)

Back view of left dress

Pale peach silk day dress with bow detailing, England, ca.1937 (p.17)

Burgundy velvet cocktail dress with short ruched sleeves, USA, ca.1938 (p.17)

Black silk crepe asymmetrical day dress, England, ca.1939 (p.18)

Purple velvet knee-length cocktail dress with structured midsection, USA, ca.1939 (p.18)

Black synthetic crepe day dress with pleated front, USA, ca.1939 (p.18)

Multicolored hand-marbled silk crepe day dress, England, ca.1939 (p.18)

Brown crepe floor-
length dress with front
swag and embroidered
neckline, USA, ca.1942
(p.19)

Sage-green printed
cotton full-skirted
dress, USA, ca.1950
(p.22)

Black taffeta full-
skirted cocktail dress
with ¾-length sleeves,
USA, ca.1957
(p.24)

Black silk chiffon
cocktail dress
with floral hemline
detailing, USA, ca.1958
(p.25)

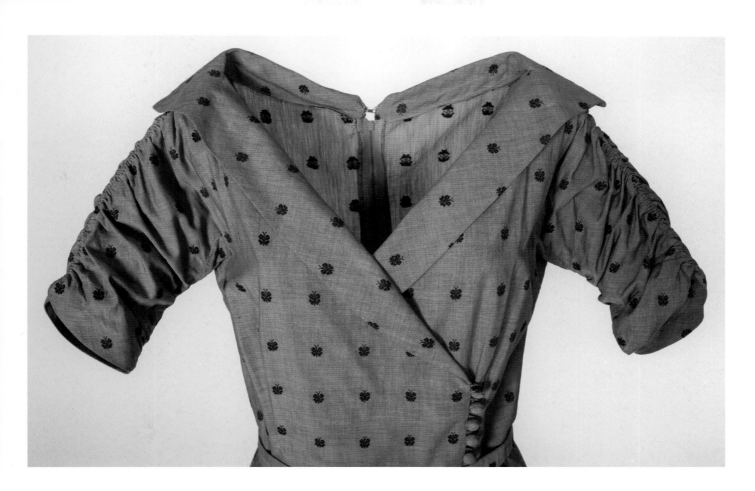

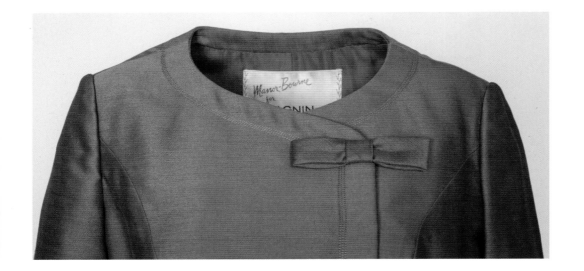

Bronze-colored
shantung skirt suit
with ¾-length sleeves,
USA, ca.1962
(p.26)

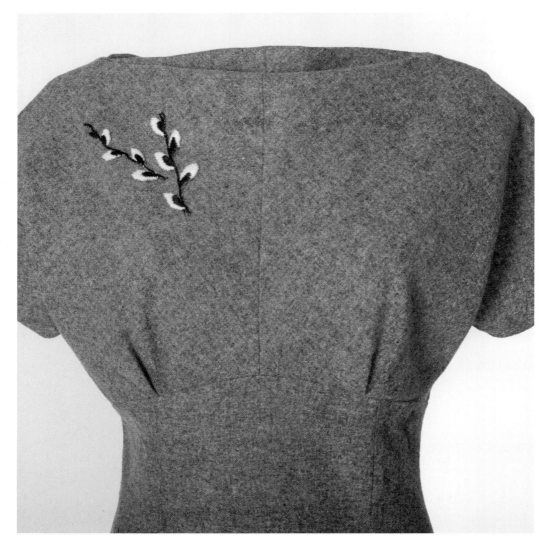

Gray wool sheath
dress embroidered
with pussy willow,
USA, ca.1963
(p.27)

Blue and white striped
full-skirted day
dress with large bow,
USA, ca.1963
(p.27)

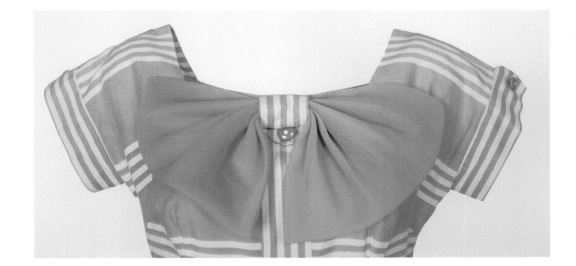

Green, white and blue
sprig-print cotton day
dress, USA, ca.1963
(p.27)

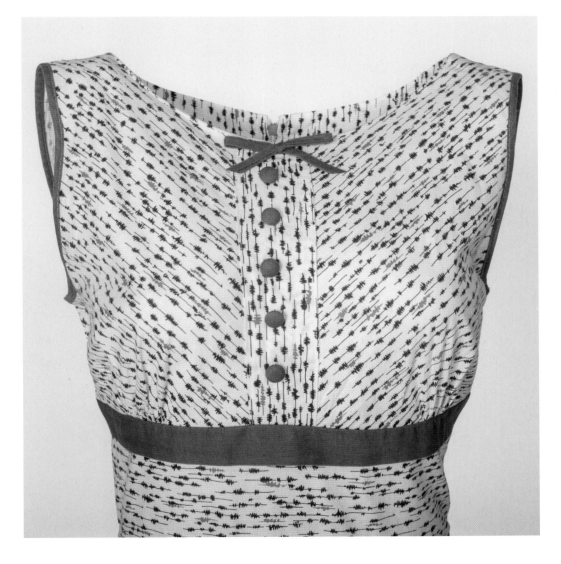

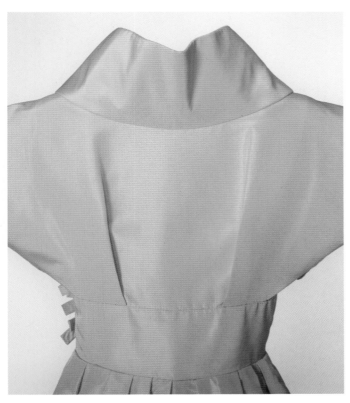

Yellow silk faille
evening dress,
USA, ca.1965
(p.27)

Back view of left dress

Bronze-colored
sleeveless cocktail
dress with
patch pockets,
Denmark, ca.1965
(p.28)

Apple-green and gold
brocade mini-cocktail
dress, USA, ca.1965
(p.28)

Cream wool collarless
cropped jacket,
USA, ca.1967
(p.30)

Camel-colored wool
collarless coat dress,
USA, ca.1967
(p.30)

Overleaf

Yellow satin long-sleeved blouse with patchwork floor-length skirt, USA, ca.1967 (p.30)

Cream heavy wool coat dress, USA, ca.1968 (p.31)

Black crepe sheath dress, USA, ca.1967 (p.29)

Ivory antique satin floor-length A-line dress, USA, ca.1969 (p.32)

White seersucker long-
sleeved minidress,
USA, ca.1969
(p.32)

Black, red, pink, blue
and yellow wool long-
sleeved ankle-length
turtleneck dress with
embroidered detailing,
USA, ca.1969
(p.32)

Green and beige
houndstooth-print
silk drop-waisted
dress with long sleeves
and jewel neckline,
USA, ca.1970
(p.33)

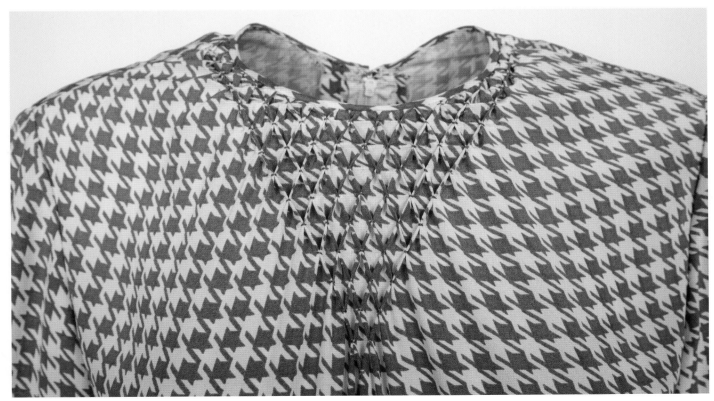

Black and yellow
printed skirt suit,
USA, ca.1970
(p.34)

Black polyester crepe
dress with lace sleeves
and rhinestone trompe
l'oeil belt, USA, ca.1975
(p.34)

Black silk satin jacket
with clover-leaf
neckline, USA, ca.1995
(p.35)

Collars

White linen jacket
with inset striped vest,
USA, ca.1914
(p.10)

Navy-blue cashmere
skirt suit with
embroidered peplum,
USA, ca.1916
(p.10)

Purple silk corduroy
skirt suit, USA, ca.1917
(p.10)

Cream cotton shirtwaist blouse with low square neckline and modified sailor collar, USA, ca.1917 (p.10)

Black and white striped faille jacket with floral-print silk lining, England, ca.1920 (p.11)

Black silk coat
with ermine trim,
USA, ca.1925
(p.12)

Natural linen
sheath dress and
jacket printed with
Art Deco motifs,
England, ca.1927
(p.13)

Dress of the outfit to
the left

Black satin coat
embellished with
cotton-floss cross
stitch in floral pattern,
USA, ca.1927
(p.13)

Black crepe evening dress with taffeta ruffles at collar, hips and cuffs, England, ca.1928 (p.13)

Back view of above dress

White and blue polka-dot cotton dress, USA, ca.1935 (p.16)

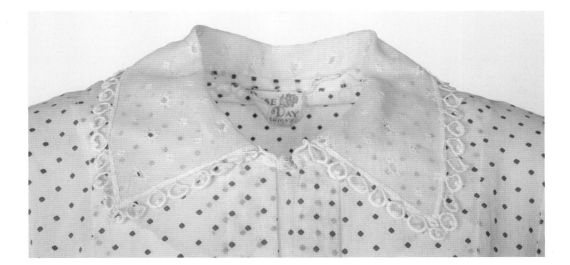

Red and pink printed cotton day dress, USA, ca.1935 (p.16)

Navy-blue wool
jacket and pants,
USA, ca.1935
(p.16)

Black velvet evening
coat with padded collar
and ruffle detailing,
USA, ca.1935
(p.16)

Spring-green bias-cut
satin evening dress,
USA, ca.1935
(p.16)

Black wool ¾-length
outerwear jacket,
USA, ca.1938
(p.17)

Blue synthetic crepe
day dress with cream
and blue lace yoke and
sleeves, USA, ca.1939
(p.18)

Black crepe long-
sleeved dress with
fringe peplum,
USA, ca.1942
(p.20)

Gray-blue wool crepe
day dress with fringe-
trimmed bound
pockets, USA, ca.1945
(p.20)

Navy-blue wool blazer with engineered stripe detailing, USA, ca.1946 (p.21)

Brown wool skirt suit, USA, ca.1947 (p.21)

Plum and gray striped wool tweed skirt suit, USA, ca.1947 (p.21)

Brown skirt suit,
USA, ca.1949
(p.21)

Pink rayon and cotton
faille housecoat,
USA, ca.1949
(p.21)

Green and navy-blue 'Black Watch' plaid shirt-jacket, USA, ca.1949 (p.21)

Purple wool flared coat with front button closure, USA, ca.1949 (p.22)

Gray wool skirt suit,
USA, ca.1950
(p.22)

Pink and gray checked
wool skirt suit,
USA, ca.1950
(p.22)

Back view of left suit

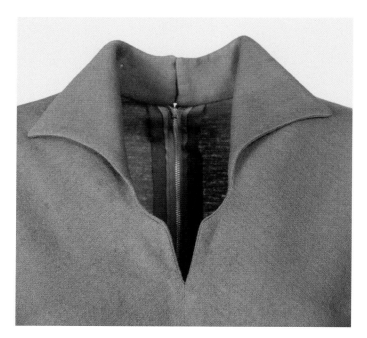

Olive-green wool
double-knit day dress,
USA, ca.1951
(p.23)

Turquoise jacket
embroidered with
toreador motifs,
Mexico, ca.1952
(p.23)

Black and brown
wool tweed jacket
with princess-seam
detailing, USA, ca.1952
(p.23)

Brown wool gabardine
car coat, USA, ca.1952
(p.23)

Brown and black
diagonal-striped wool
coat, USA, ca.1955
(p.24)

Black cashmere jacket
with matching belt
and ¾-length sleeves,
USA, ca.1955
(p.24)

Black velvet ¾-length
swing coat with
¾-length sleeves,
USA, ca.1957
(p.25)

Oatmeal-colored
heavy wool bolero,
USA, ca.1957
(p.25)

Taupe silk cocktail
dress, USA, ca.1958
(p.25)

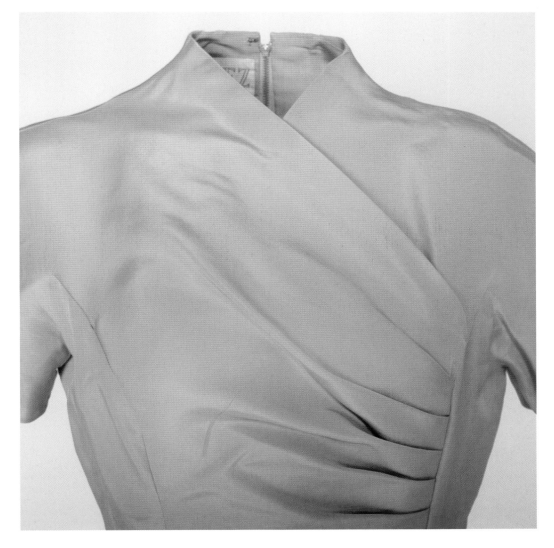

Navy-blue and white
silk novelty-weave skirt
suit, USA, ca.1960
(p.26)

Overleaf

Red wool double-breasted day suit, USA, ca.1962 (p.26)

Pink and white patterned scoop-necked dress with matching short jacket, USA, ca.1965 (p.27)

Oatmeal-colored wool evening dress and matching jacket with hot-pink rhinestone buttons, USA, ca.1965 (p.28)

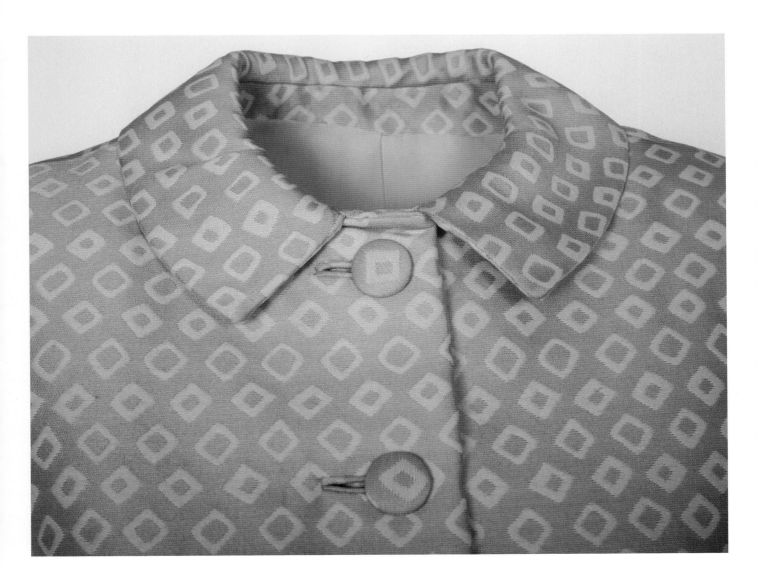

Cream wool crepe
sheath dress with
matching coat,
trimmed in pink wool,
France, ca.1965
(p.28)

Brown crepe long-sleeved tunic with sequined bands on center front and cuffs, France, ca.1966 (p.29)

Gray wool long-sleeved dress with pink velvet bow and cream satin collar and cuffs, USA, ca.1968 (p.31)

Cream and turquoise
wool sleeveless sheath
dress, France, ca.1967
(p.30)

Red and cream
printed silk twill
long-sleeved dress
with mock turtleneck,
USA, ca.1967
(p.30)

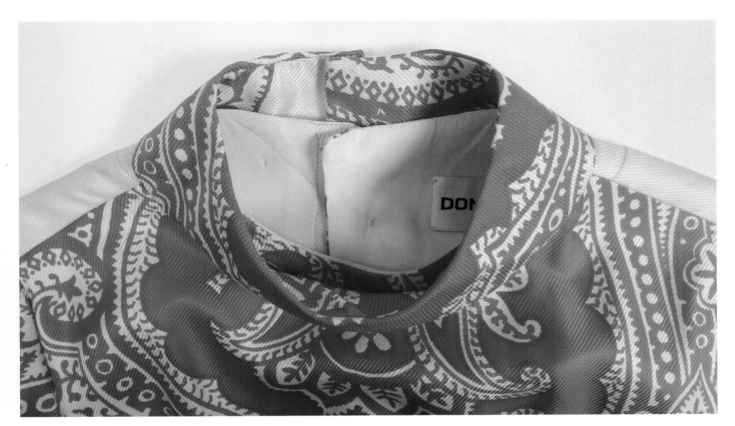

COLLARS

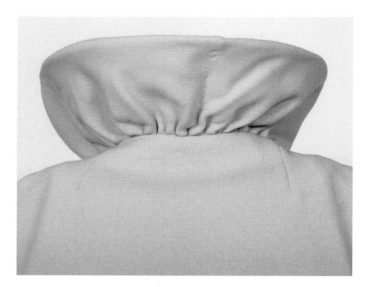

Greige wool crepe
sleeveless mini-
cocktail dress
with ruffle trim,
USA, ca.1968
(p.28)

Back view of left dress

VINTAGE DETAILS

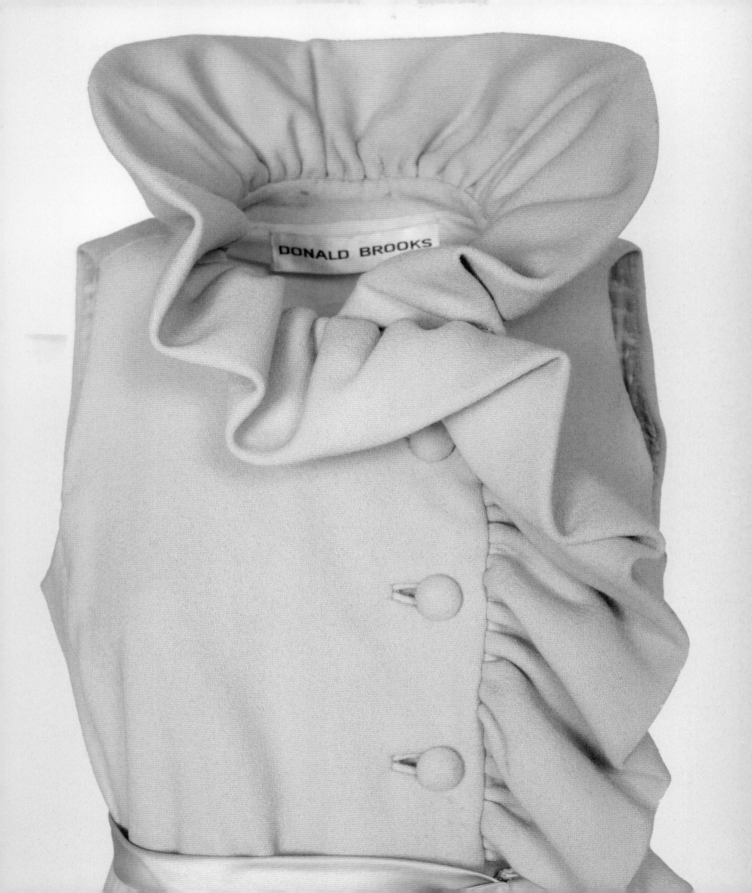

Orange Art-Deco-print chiffon long-sleeved sheath dress, USA, ca.1968 (p.31)

Back view of above dress

Black asymmetrical
wool jacket with
single-button closure,
USA, ca.1968
(p.31)

Black silk faille
¾-length jacket, USA,
ca.1968
(p.31)

White and black
silk dress trimmed
with silver studs,
USA, ca.1969
(p.33)

Taupe sleeveless
sheath dress with
matching long-sleeved
coat, USA, ca.1969
(p.32)

Turquoise wool double-
breasted skirt suit,
France, ca.1970
(p.33)

Navy-blue and white
speckled wool tweed
skirt suit, USA, ca.1970
(p.34)

Purple and white
checked wool
long-sleeved dress
with flared skirt,
USA, ca.1970
(p.34)

Brown cotton velveteen
double-breasted
jacket trimmed with
brown wool flannel,
USA, ca.1971
(p.34)

Dark purple wool coat,
USA, ca.1975
(p.34)

Cream wool double-
knit long-sleeved day
dress with brown
synthetic leather
piping, USA, ca.1983
(p.35)

Black wool waist-length
jacket, USA, ca.1994
(p.35)

Black silk satin ruffle-
pocket jacket, USA,
ca.1995
(p.35)

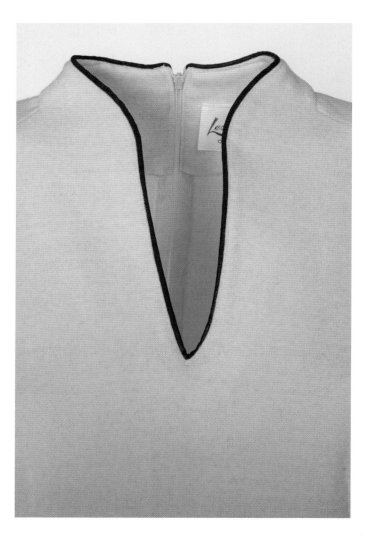

CONOVER MAYER

6

Sleeves

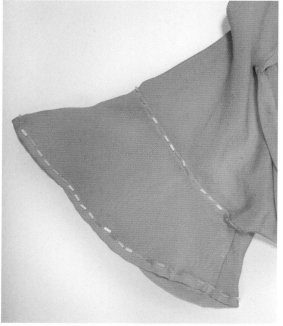

Cream silk short-
sleeved day dress with
cream lace overskirt,
USA, ca.1920
(p.10)

Brown silk georgette
day dress with
turquoise and brown
satin ribbon bows,
USA, ca.1922
(p.11)

Back view of left dress

SLEEVES

Silver lace dress
over cream silk
taffeta underdress,
USA, ca.1923
(p.11)

Rose-pink chiffon long-
sleeved knee-length
dress with cream lace
inset at front, sleeves
and hem, USA, ca.1925
(p.12)

Purple devoré coat,
USA, ca.1926
(p.12)

Black satin long-
sleeved evening dress
with cream lace sleeve
and hem detailing,
USA, ca.1927
(p.13)

Black wool crepe day
dress with black devoré
sleeves and collar,
USA, ca.1932
(p.14)

Red and pink printed
cotton day dress,
USA, ca.1935
(p.16)

Back view of left dress

Black crepe dress with
circular ruffled sleeves
lined in white faille,
USA, ca.1935
(p.15)

Purple velvet floor-
length evening dress,
USA, ca.1935
(p.15)

Spring-green bias-cut satin evening dress, USA, ca.1935 (p.15)

White cotton eyelet-embroidered dress with cape collar, USA, ca.1935 (p.15)

Back view of left dress

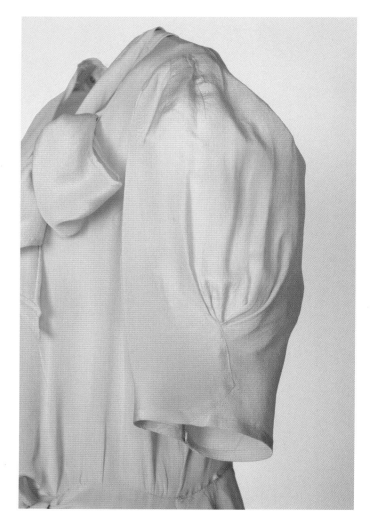

Pale peach silk
day dress with
bow detailing,
England, ca.1937
(p.17)

Burgundy velvet
cocktail dress with
short ruched sleeves,
USA, ca.1938
(p.17)

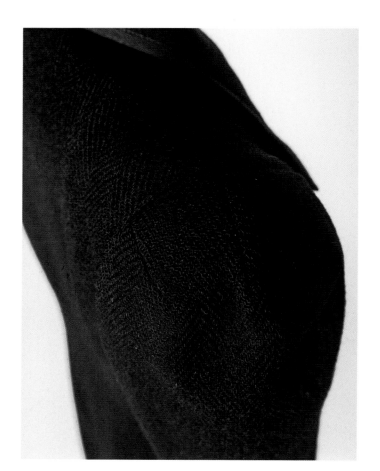

Black wool ¾-length
outerwear jacket,
USA, ca.1938
(p.17)

Multicolored hand-
marbled silk crepe day
dress, England, ca.1939
(p.18)

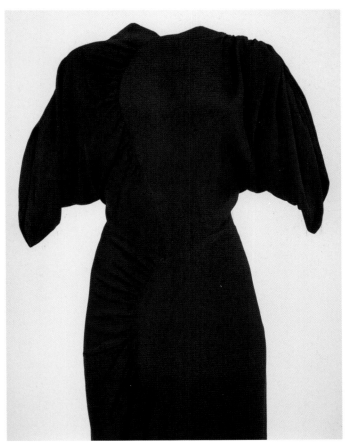

Burgundy velvet
cocktail dress with
beaded bow trim,
USA, ca.1939
(p.17)

Black silk crepe
asymmetrical day
dress, England, ca.1939
(p.18)

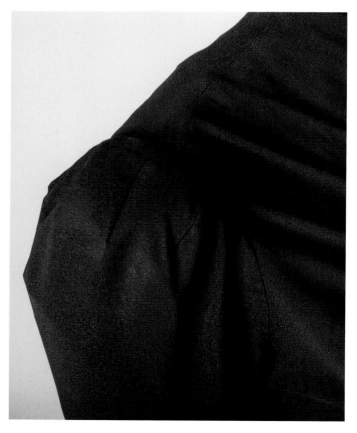

Black synthetic crepe
day dress with pleated
front, USA, ca.1939
(p.18)

Gray and black printed
nylon day dress,
USA, ca.1939
(p.18)

Purple velvet knee-
length cocktail dress
with structured
midsection,
USA, ca.1939
(p.18)

Brown wool skirt
suit, USA, ca.1947
(back view)
(p.21)

Pink rayon and cotton
faille housecoat,
USA, ca.1949
(p.21)

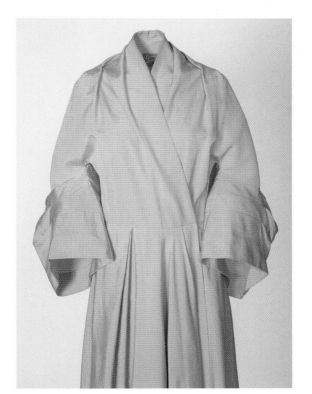

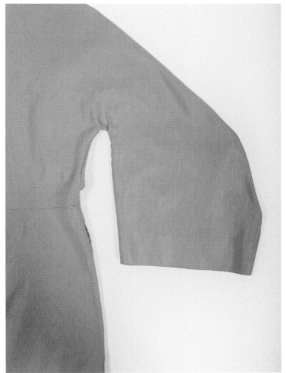

Green and navy-
blue 'Black Watch'
plaid shirt-jacket,
USA, ca.1949
(p.21)

Sage-green printed
cotton full-skirted
dress, USA, ca.1950
(p.22)

Black cashmere jacket
with matching belt
and ¾-length sleeves,
USA, ca.1955
(p.24)

Blue and white striped
full-skirted day
dress with large bow,
USA, ca.1963
(p.27)

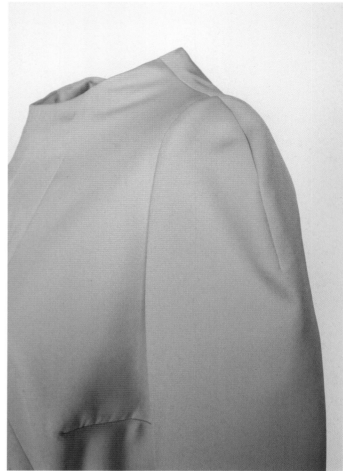

Black synthetic crepe
sheath dress with full-
length organza lantern
sleeves, USA, ca.1965
(p.27)

Yellow satin long-
sleeved blouse with
patchwork floor-length
skirt, USA, ca.1967
(p.30)

VINTAGE DETAILS

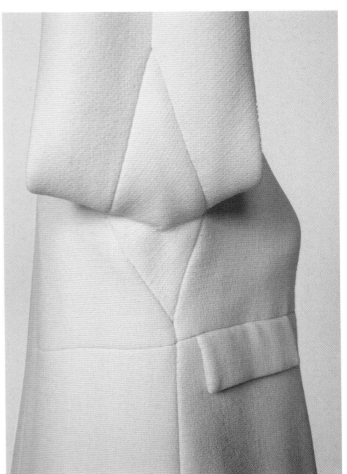

Cream heavy wool coat
dress, USA, ca.1968
(p.31)

Black, red, pink, blue and yellow wool long-sleeved ankle-length turtleneck dress with embroidered detailing, USA, ca.1969 (p.32)

Black velvet jumpsuit
with appliquéd
organdie sleeves and
hem, USA, ca.1969
(back view)
(p.32)

White seersucker long-
sleeved minidress,
USA, ca.1969
(p.32)

Cream wool double-
knit long-sleeved day
dress with brown
synthetic leather
piping, USA, ca.1983
(p.35)

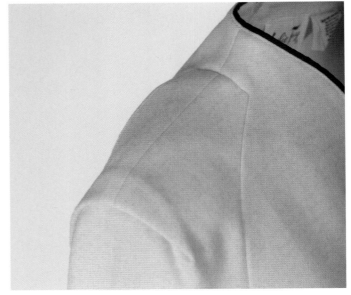

Turquoise silk charmeuse batwing dress, China, ca.1985 (p.35)

Cream wool challis bodice with long sleeves and circular peplum, USA, ca.1985 (p.35)

Black silk satin ruffle-
pocket jacket, USA,
ca.1995
(p.35)

Black silk satin jacket
with clover-leaf
neckline, USA, ca.1995
(p.35)

Cuffs

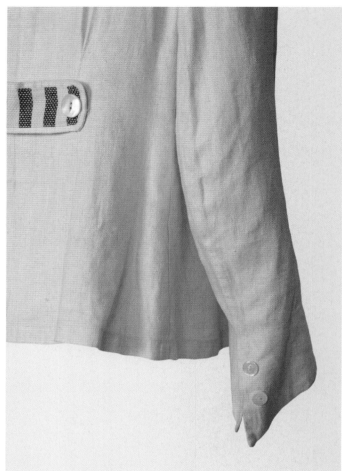

Hot-pink velveteen
jacket with soutache
trim and silk
floss embroidery,
Italy, ca.1913 (back view)
(p.10)

White linen jacket with
inset striped vest, USA,
ca.1914 (back view)
(p.10)

Navy-blue cashmere
skirt suit with
embroidered peplum,
USA, ca.1916
(p.10)

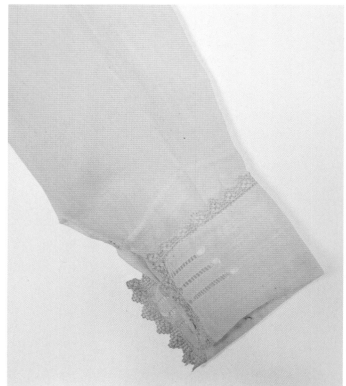

Purple silk corduroy
skirt suit, USA, ca.1917
(p.10)

Cream cotton
shirtwaist blouse with
low square neckline
and modified sailor
collar, USA, ca.1917
(p.10)

Black and white striped
faille jacket with
floral-print silk lining,
England, ca.1920
(back view)
(p.11)

Black silk coat
with ermine trim,
USA, ca.1925
(p.12)

Cream georgette
dress and jacket,
USA, ca.1927
(p.12)

Back view of left dress
and jacket

Oyster-colored silk
crepe long-sleeved
asymmetrical day
dress, USA, ca.1927
(p.13)

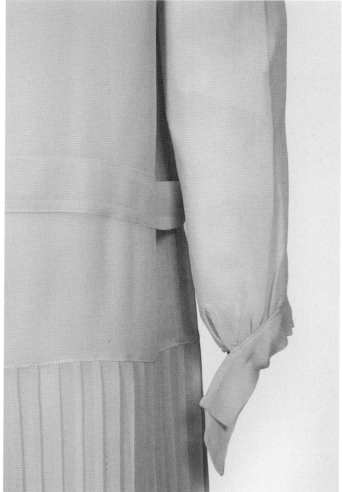

Black satin coat
embellished with
cotton-floss cross
stitch in floral pattern,
USA, ca.1927
(p.13)

Black crepe evening
dress with taffeta
ruffles at collar,
hips and cuffs,
England, ca.1928
(p.13)

Black wool crepe day dress with black devoré sleeves and collar, USA, ca.1932 (p.14)

White and blue polka-dot cotton dress, USA, ca.1935 (p.16)

Black velvet evening coat with padded collar and ruffle detailing, USA, ca.1935 (p.16)

Black wool ¾-length outerwear jacket, USA, ca.1938 (p.17)

Gray wool skirt suit,
USA, ca.1950
(p.22)

Navy-blue silk
taffeta shirt dress,
USA, ca.1950
(p.22)

Pink and gray checked
wool skirt suit, USA,
ca.1950 (back view)
(p.22)

Olive-green wool
double-knit day dress,
USA, ca.1951
(p.23)

Black velvet ¾-length
swing coat with
¾-length sleeves,
USA, ca.1957
(p.25)

Oatmeal-colored
heavy wool bolero,
USA, ca.1957
(back view)
(p.25)

Red wool double-breasted day suit, USA, ca.1962 (p.26)

Oatmeal-colored wool
evening dress and
matching jacket with
hot-pink rhinestone
buttons, USA, ca.1965
(p.28)

Black synthetic crepe
sheath dress with full-
length organza lantern
sleeves, USA, ca.1965
(p.27)

Brown crepe long-sleeved tunic with sequined bands on center front and cuffs, France, ca.1966 (p.29)

Red and cream printed silk twill long-sleeved dress with mock turtleneck, USA, ca.1967 (back view) (p.30)

Cream silk tunic with beaded bib and cuffs, USA, ca.1968 (p.31)

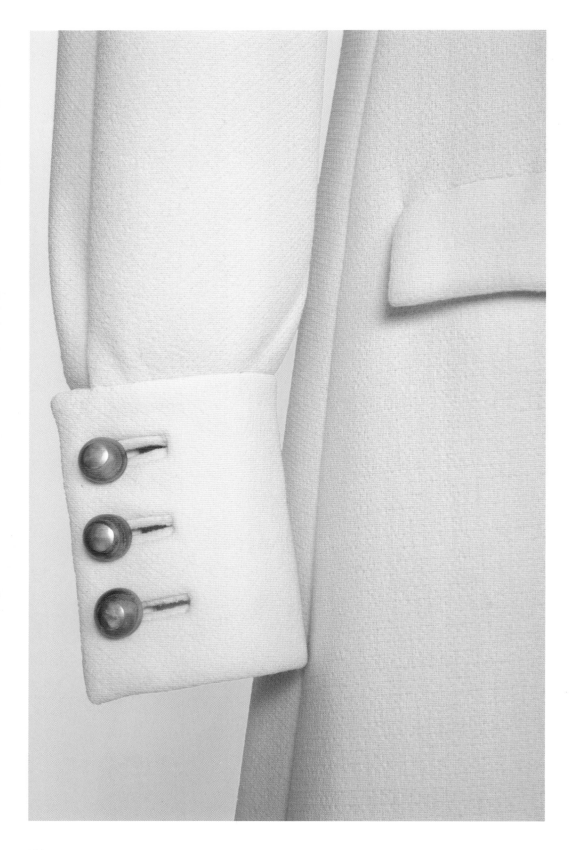

Cream heavy wool coat
dress, USA, ca.1968
(p.31)

Green and beige
houndstooth-print
silk drop-waisted
dress with long sleeves
and jewel neckline,
USA, ca.1970
(p.33)

Back view of left dress

Brown cotton velveteen double-breasted jacket trimmed with brown wool flannel, USA, ca.1971 (p.34)

Dark purple wool coat, USA, ca.1975 (p.34)

Cream wool challis bodice with long sleeves and circular peplum, USA, ca.1985 (p.35)

Pockets

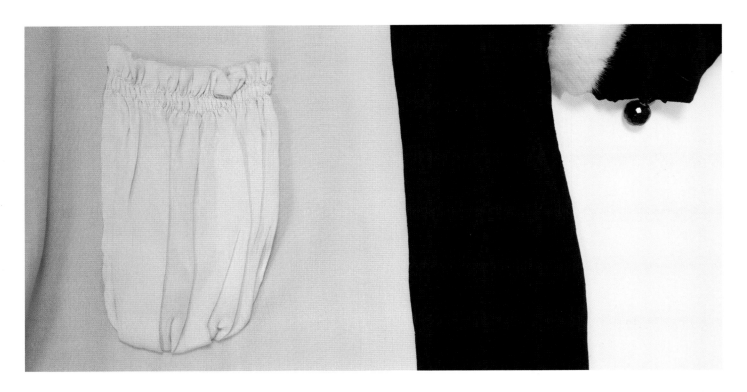

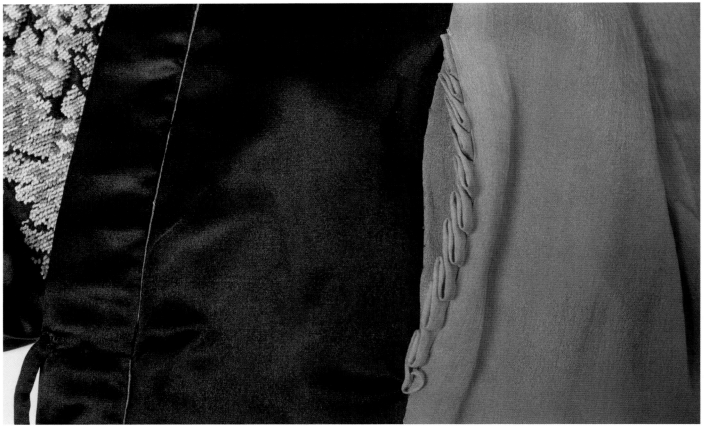

Black silk coat
with ermine trim,
USA, ca.1925
(p.12)

Black satin coat
embellished with
cotton-floss cross
stitch in floral pattern,
USA, ca.1927
(p.13)

Blue, yellow and red
paisley-print cotton
voile day dress with
drawstring pockets,
USA, ca.1932
(p.14)

Red and pink printed
cotton day dress,
USA, ca.1935
(p.16)

Black wool ¾-length
outerwear jacket,
USA, ca.1938
(p.17)

Red wool tweed blazer,
USA, ca.1944
(p.20)

Gray-blue wool crepe
day dress with fringe-
trimmed bound
pockets, USA, ca.1945
(p.20)

Plum and gray striped
wool tweed skirt suit,
USA, ca.1947
(p.21)

Red wool felt circle skirt with black braid and embroidery decoration, USA, ca.1950 (p.22)

Gray wool skirt suit,
USA, ca.1950
(p.22)

Gray wool day skirt
with V-shaped pocket,
USA, ca.1952
(p.23)

Dark-gray wool A-line
skirt with light-gray hip
pockets, USA, ca.1955
(p.23)

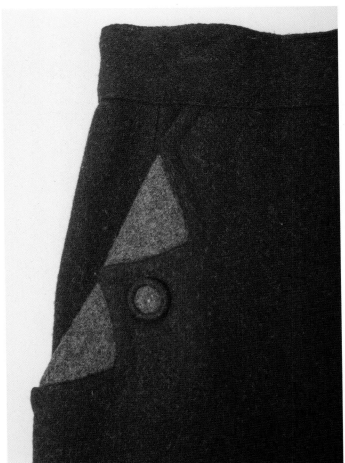

Brown and black
diagonal-striped wool
coat, USA, ca.1955
(p.24)

Navy-blue and white
silk novelty-weave skirt
suit, USA, ca.1960
(p.26)

Red silk shantung
dress with matching
bolero, USA, ca.1960
(p.26)

Bronze-colored
sleeveless cocktail
dress with
patch pockets,
Denmark, ca.1965
(p.28)

Black crepe sheath
dress, USA, ca.1967
(p.29)

Camel-colored wool
collarless coat dress,
USA, ca.1967
(p.30)

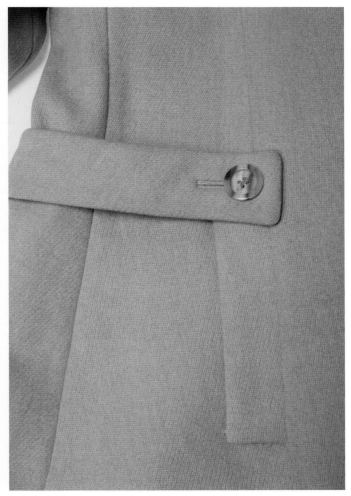

Cream and turquoise
wool sleeveless sheath
dress, France, ca.1967
(p.30)

Black asymmetrical
wool jacket with
single-button closure,
USA, ca.1968
(p.31)

Taupe sleeveless
sheath dress with
matching long-sleeved
coat, USA, ca.1969
(p.32)

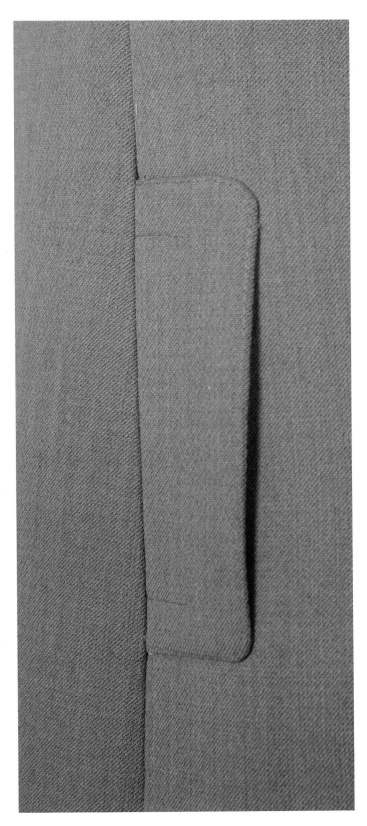

Navy-blue and white speckled wool tweed skirt suit, USA, ca.1970 (p.34)

Cream and eggplant-colored triangle-print tunic and skirt ensemble, USA, ca.1970 (p.33)

Black and yellow printed skirt suit, USA, ca.1970 (p.34)

Turquoise wool double-
breasted skirt suit,
France, ca.1970
(p.33)

Dark purple wool coat,
USA, ca.1975
(p.34)

Cream wool double-
knit long-sleeved day
dress with brown
synthetic leather
piping, USA, ca.1983
(p.35)

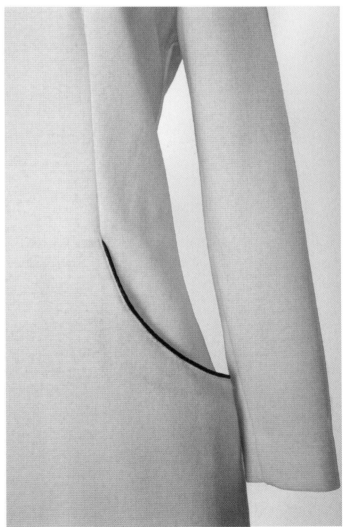

Turquoise silk
charmeuse batwing
dress, China, ca.1985
(p.35)

Black wool waist-length
jacket, USA, ca.1994
(p.35)

Black silk satin ruffle-
pocket jacket, USA,
ca.1995
(p.35)

Fastenings & Buttonholes

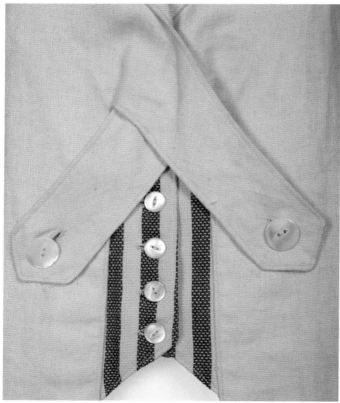

White linen jacket
with inset striped
vest, USA, ca.1914
(p.10)

Navy-blue cashmere
skirt suit with
embroidered peplum,
USA, ca.1916
(p.10)

Purple silk corduroy
skirt suit, USA, ca.1917
(p.10)

Back view of above suit

Black and white striped
faille jacket with
floral-print silk lining,
England, ca.1920
(p.11)

Cream silk short-
sleeved day dress with
cream lace overskirt,
USA, ca.1920
(back view)
(p.10)

Brown silk georgette
day dress with
turquoise and brown
satin ribbon bows, USA,
ca.1922 (back view)
(p.11)

Robin's-egg-blue silk
taffeta sleeveless *robe
de style*, USA, ca.1924
(p.11)

Ivory silk sleeveless
sheath dress with
lace flounced skirt,
USA, ca.1924
(p.12)

Natural linen
sheath dress and
jacket printed with
Art Deco motifs,
England, ca.1927
(p.13)

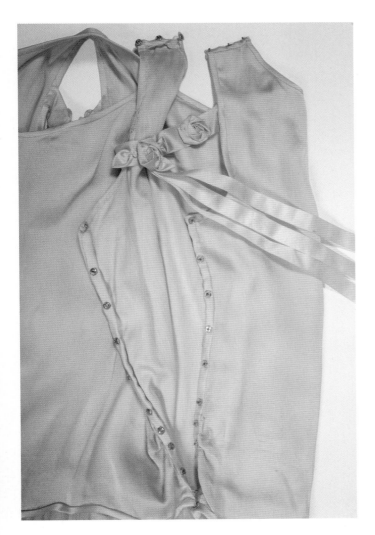

White silk taffeta and silk net party dress, USA, ca.1929 (p.13)

Fuchsia silk georgette day dress embellished with horizontal, pleated ruffles, USA, ca.1930 (p.14)

White and blue polka-dot cotton dress, USA, ca.1935 (p.16)

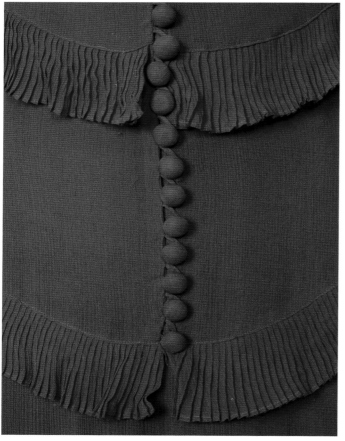

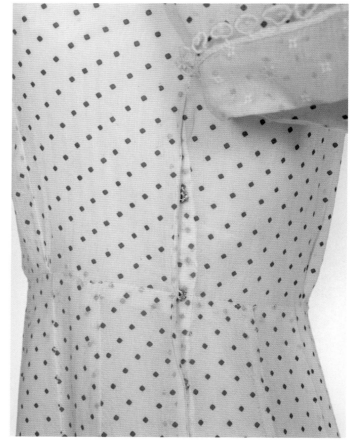

Black crepe dress with
circular ruffled sleeves
lined in white faille,
USA, ca.1935
(back view)
(p.15)

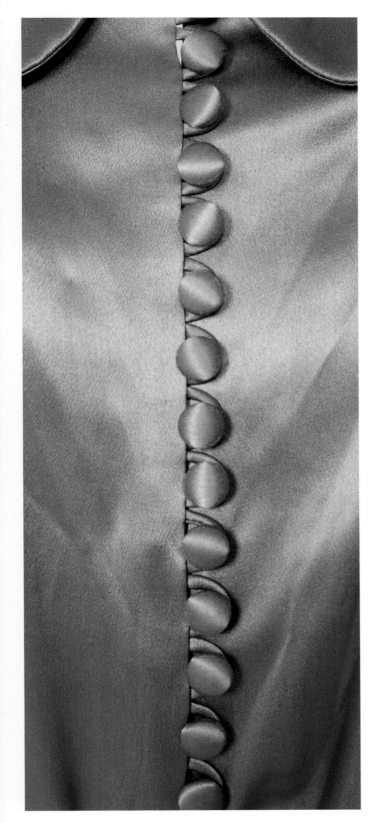

Green chenille knitted
dress with ¾-length
skirt and sleeves,
USA, ca.1935 (back
view) (p.15)

Spring-green bias-cut
satin evening dress,
USA, ca.1935
(back view)
(p.16)

Black synthetic crepe
day dress with pleated
front, USA, ca.1939
(back view)
(p.18)

Orange and brown
plaid wool outerwear
jacket, USA, ca.1940
(p.19)

Black crepe long-
sleeved dress with
fringe peplum,
USA, ca.1942
(p.20)

Brown crepe short-
sleeved cocktail dress,
USA, ca.1942
(back view)
(p.20)

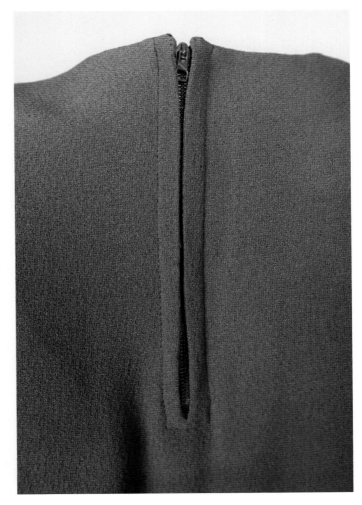

Red wool tweed blazer,
USA, ca.1944
(p.20)

White rayon short-
sleeved blouse with
red hand-stitching,
USA, ca.1945
(p.20)

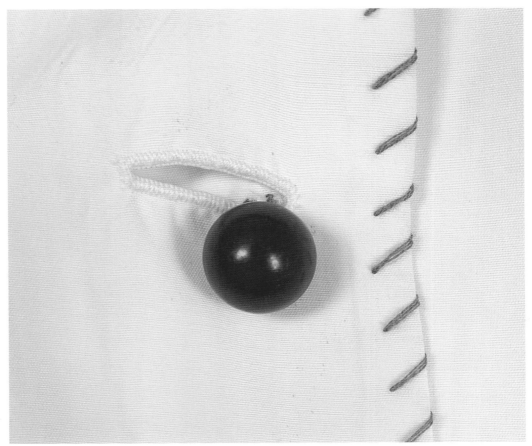

Navy-blue wool blazer
with engineered stripe
detailing, USA, ca.1946
(p.21)

Brown wool skirt suit,
USA, ca.1947
(p.21)

Purple wool flared
coat with front button
closure, USA, ca.1949
(p.22)

Sage-green printed
cotton full-skirted
dress, USA, ca.1950
(p.22)

Olive-green wool
double-knit day dress,
USA, ca.1951 (back
view) (p.23)

Below left and overleaf

Brown wool gabardine car coat, USA, ca.1952 (p.23)

Cream satin ¾-length sleeve cocktail dress brocaded with green and pink motifs, and green bow at bust, USA, ca.1956 (p.24)

Black silk chiffon full-skirted cocktail dress, USA, ca.1958 (back view) (p.25)

VINTAGE DETAILS

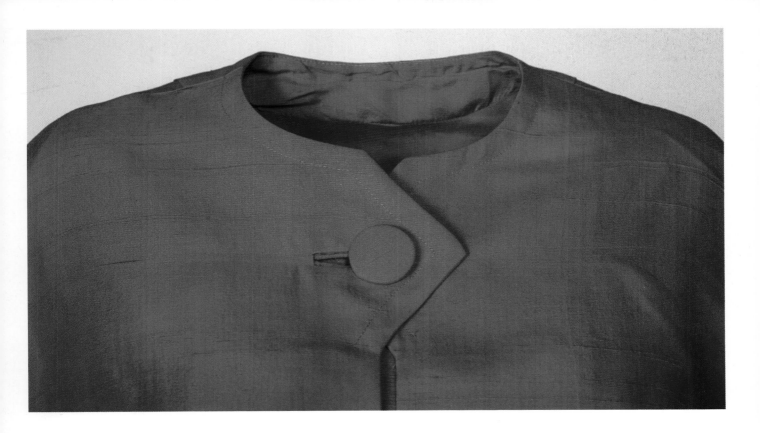

Turquoise silk satin
two-piece sheath
evening dress,
USA, ca.1960 (back
view) (p.25)

Red silk shantung
dress with matching
bolero, USA, ca.1960
(p.26)

Oatmeal-colored
wool short-sleeved
day dress with
separate back panel,
France(?), ca.1962
(back view) (p.26)

Bronze-colored
sleeveless cocktail
dress with
patch pockets,
Denmark, ca.1965
(back view) (p.28)

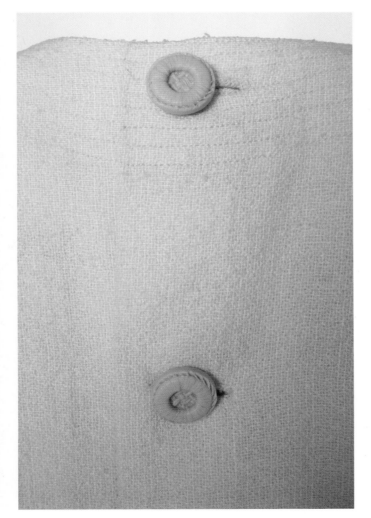

Pink and white
patterned scoop-
necked dress with
matching short jacket,
USA, ca.1965
(p.27)

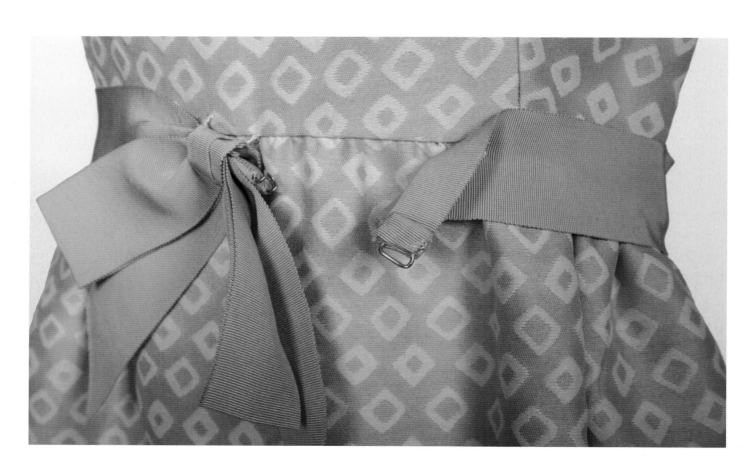

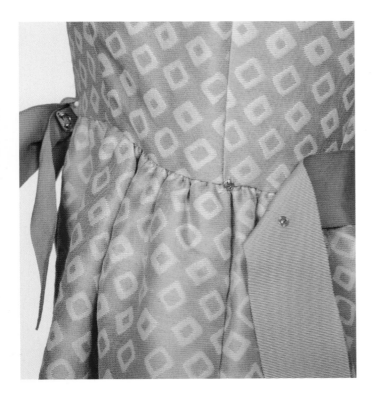

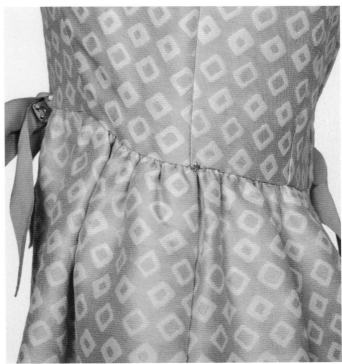

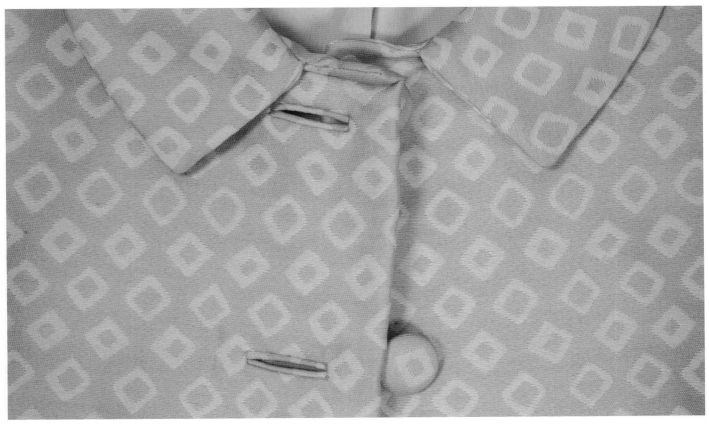

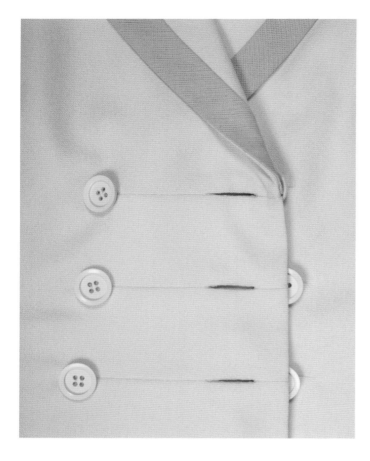

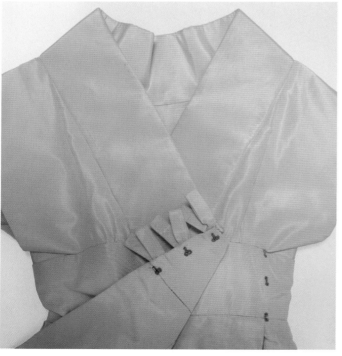

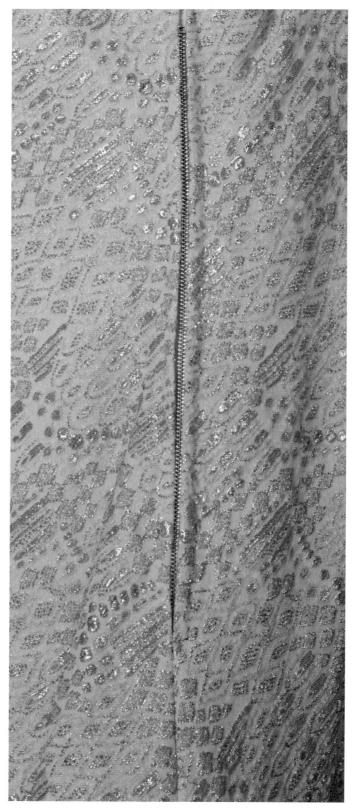

Cream wool crepe
sheath dress with
matching coat,
trimmed in pink wool,
France, ca.1965
(p.28)

Yellow silk faille
evening dress,
USA, ca.1965
(p.27)

Apple-green and gold
brocade mini-cocktail
dress, USA, ca.1965
(p.28)

Cream wool collarless
cropped jacket,
USA, ca.1967
(p.30)

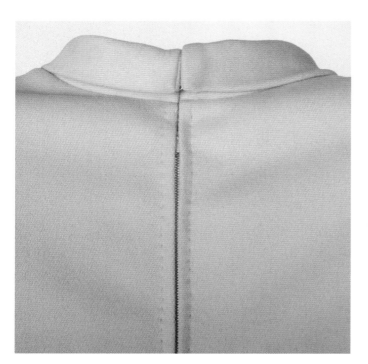

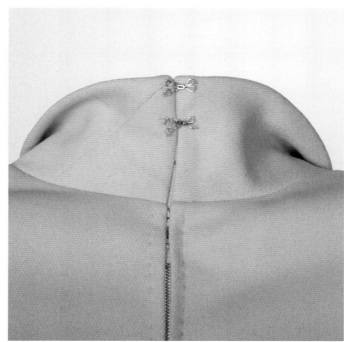

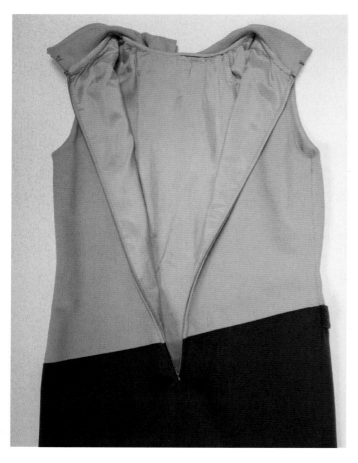

Cream and turquoise
wool sleeveless sheath
dress, France, ca.1967
(back view)
(p.30)

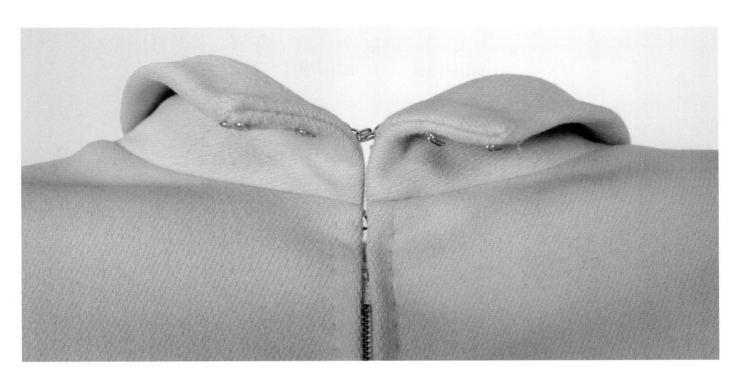

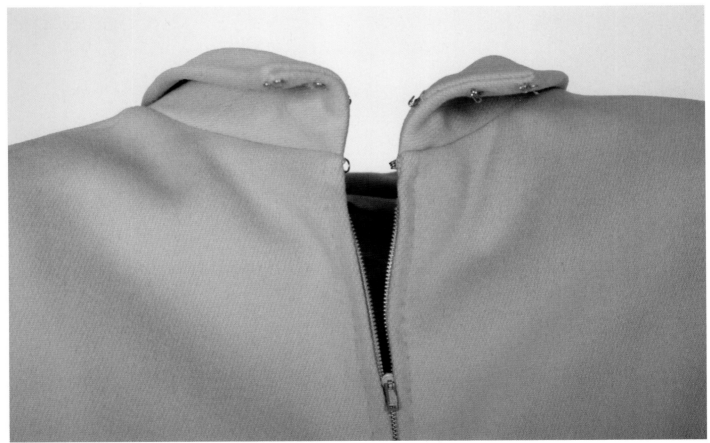

Yellow satin long-
sleeved blouse with
patchwork floor-length
skirt, USA, ca.1967
(back view) (p.30)

Camel-colored wool
collarless coat dress,
USA, ca.1967
(p.30)

Cream heavy wool coat
dress, USA, ca.1968
(p.31)

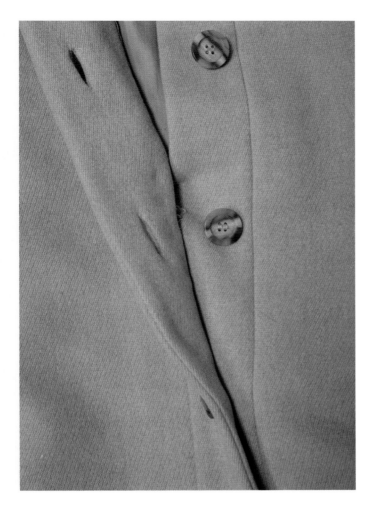

Greige wool crepe
sleeveless mini-
cocktail dress
with ruffle trim,
USA, ca.1968
(p.30)

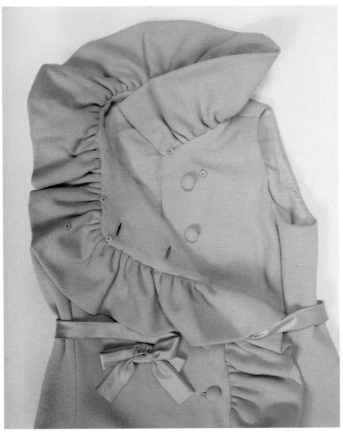

Black asymmetrical wool jacket with single-button closure, USA, ca.1968 (p.31)

Ivory antique satin floor-length A-line dress, USA, ca.1969 (back view) (p.32)

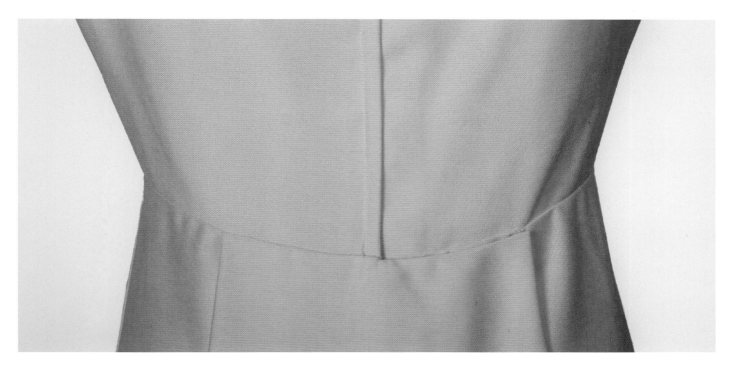

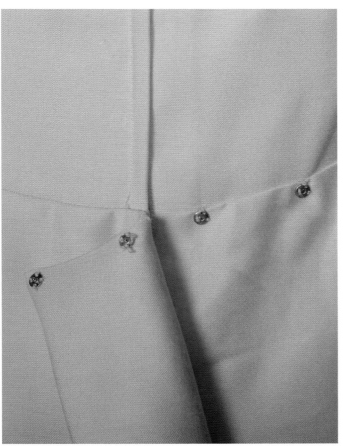

Taupe sleeveless
sheath dress with
matching long-sleeved
coat, USA, ca.1969
(dress only, back view)
(p.32)

White and black
silk dress trimmed
with silver studs,
USA, ca.1969
(p.33)

Green and beige
houndstooth-print
silk drop-waisted
dress with long sleeves
and jewel neckline,
USA, ca.1970
(p.33)

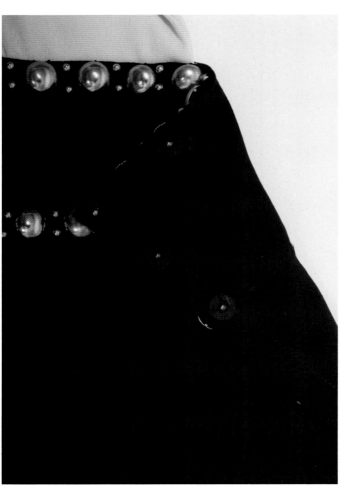

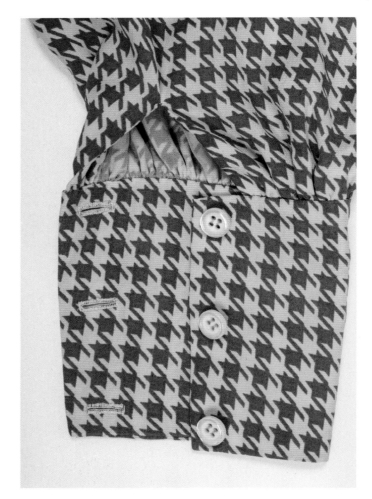

Black silk satin jacket with clover-leaf neckline, USA, ca.1995 (p.35)

Hems, Darts, Stitching & Fitting Devices

Black and white striped faille jacket with floral-print silk lining, England, ca.1920 (p.11)

Back view of left jacket

Silver lace dress
over cream silk
taffeta underdress,
USA, ca.1923
(p.11)

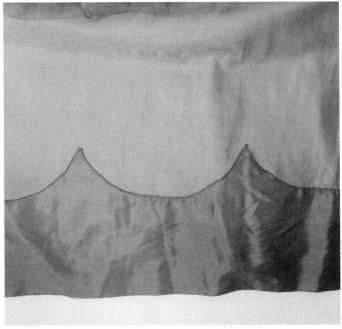

Robin's-egg-blue silk taffeta sleeveless *robe de style*, USA, ca.1924 (p.11)

Black velvet *robe de style* with jagged hem and poppy trim, USA, ca.1924 (p.11)

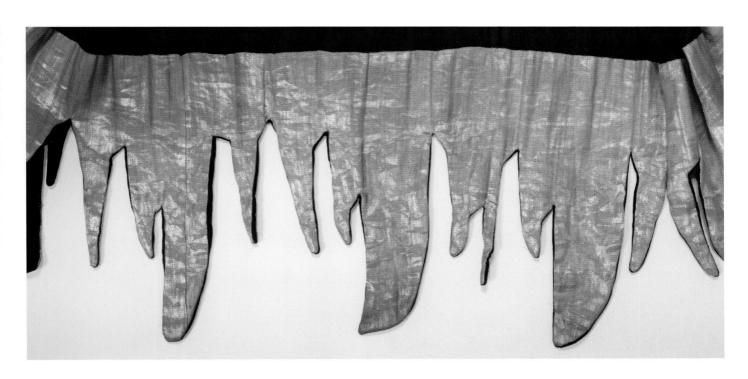

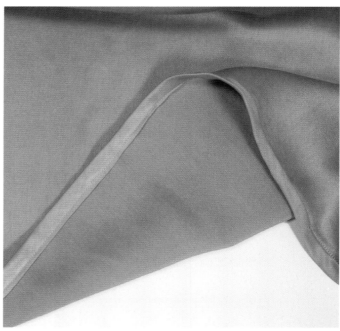

VINTAGE DETAILS

Black satin long-sleeved evening dress with cream lace sleeve and hem detailing, USA, ca.1927 (p.13)

Oyster-colored silk crepe long-sleeved asymmetrical day dress, USA, ca.1927 (p.13)

Natural linen sheath dress and jacket printed with Art Deco motifs, England, ca.1927 (back view) (p.13)

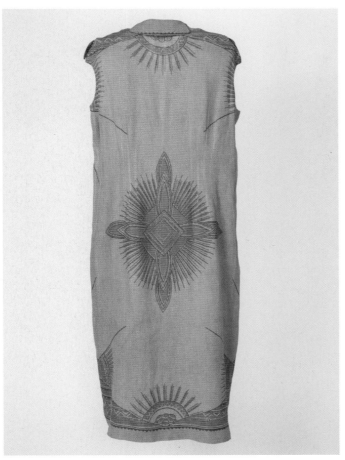

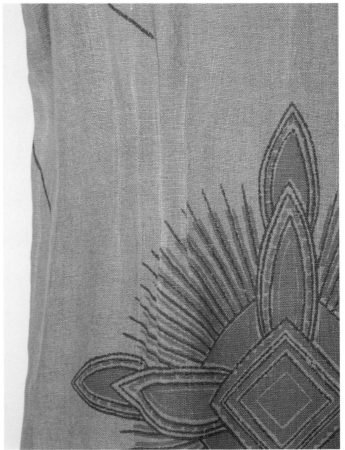

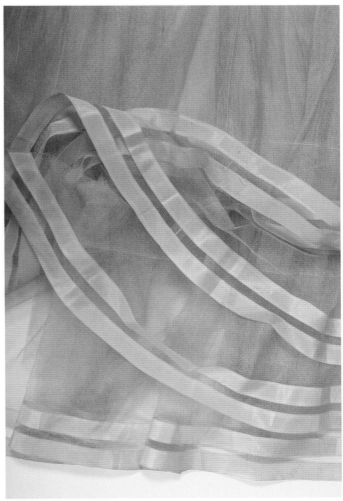

White silk taffeta and
silk net party dress,
USA, ca.1929
(p.13)

Back view of left dress

Black velvet evening
coat with padded collar
and ruffle detailing,
USA, ca.1935
(p.16)

Floral-print chiffon
dress with ruffles at
neckline and hem,
USA, ca.1935
(p.14)

Spring-green bias-cut
satin evening dress,
USA, ca.1935
(p.16)

Black and white
micro-polka-dot silk
charmeuse evening
dress, USA, ca.1935
(p.15)

Purple velvet floor-
length evening dress,
USA, ca.1935
(p.15)

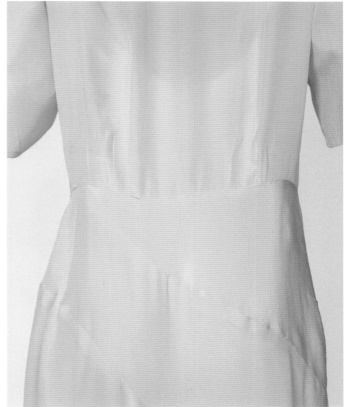

Pale peach silk
day dress with
bow detailing,
England, ca.1937
(p.17)

Back view of left dress

Black wool ¾-length
outerwear jacket,
USA, ca.1938
(back view) (p.17)

Black silk crepe asymmetrical day dress, England, ca.1939 (p.18)

Blue synthetic crepe day dress with cream and blue lace yoke and sleeves, USA, ca.1939 (p.18)

Blue, pink and white
floral-print day dress,
USA, ca.1940
(p.18)

VINTAGE DETAILS

White rayon short-sleeved blouse with red hand-stitching, USA, ca.1945 (p.20)

Navy-blue wool blazer with engineered stripe detailing, USA, ca.1946 (p.21)

Brown wool skirt suit, USA, ca.1947 (p.21)

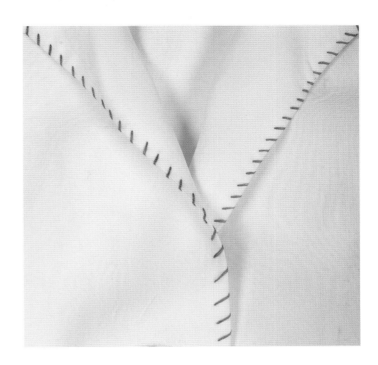

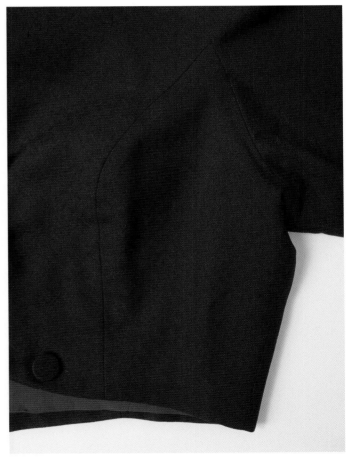

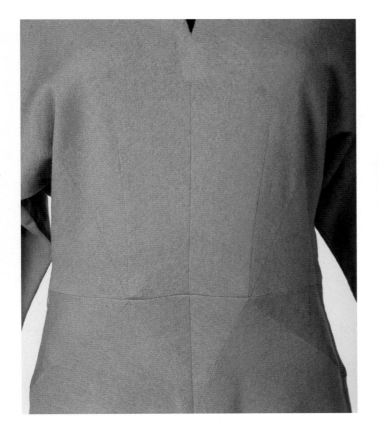

Purple wool flared
coat with front button
closure, USA, ca.1949
(p.22)

Back view of left coat

Olive-green wool
double-knit day dress,
USA, ca.1951
(p.23)

Black and brown
wool tweed jacket
with princess-seam
detailing, USA, ca.1952
(p.23)

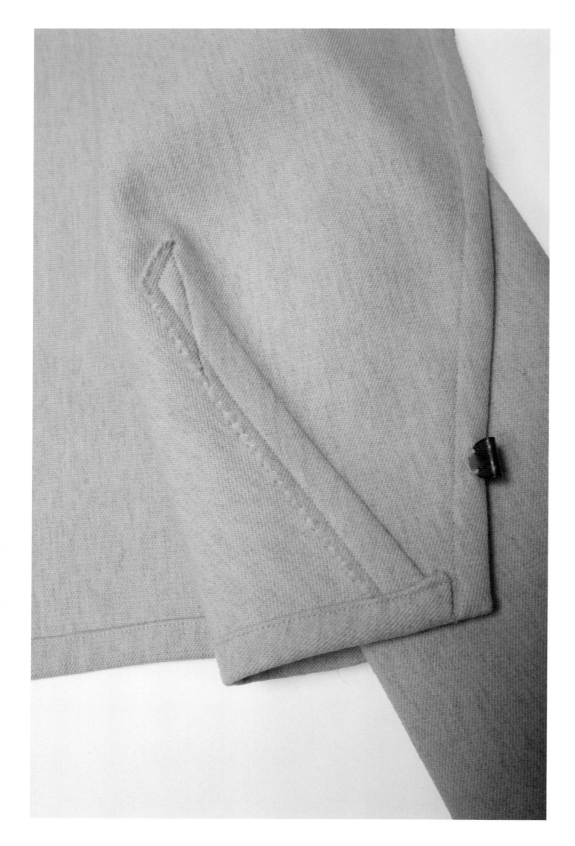

Oatmeal-colored
heavy wool bolero,
USA, ca.1957
(p.25)

Back view of left bolero

Black taffeta full-
skirted cocktail dress
with ¾-length sleeves,
USA, ca.1957
(p.24)

Back view of left dress

Oatmeal-colored
wool short-sleeved
day dress with
separate back panel,
France(?), ca.1962
(p.26)

Bronze-colored
shantung skirt suit
with ¾-length sleeves,
USA, ca.1962
(p.26)

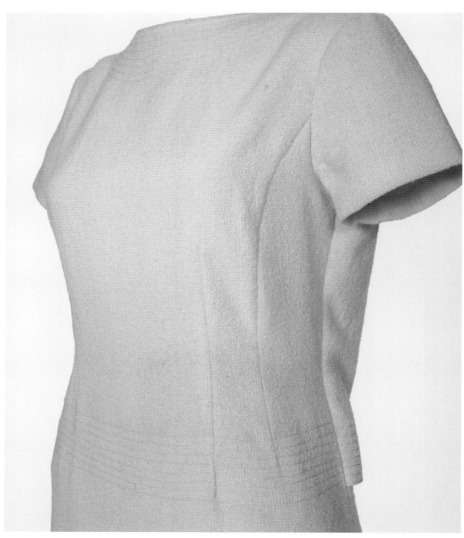

Gray wool sheath
dress embroidered
with pussy willow,
USA, ca.1963
(p.27)

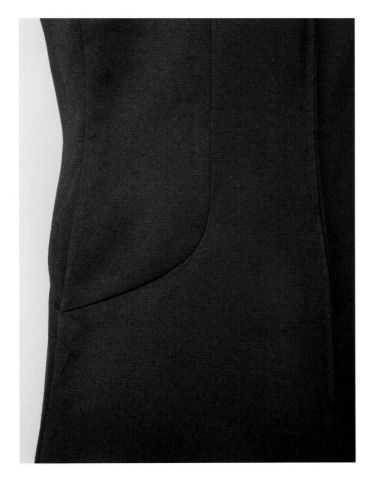

Above, right and overleaf

Black synthetic satin
sleeveless sheath
dress with scalloped,
pleated ruffle at hem,
USA, ca.1965
(p.28)

Back view of left dress

Apple-green and gold brocade mini-cocktail dress, USA, ca.1965 (p.28)

Black synthetic crepe
sheath dress with full-
length organza lantern
sleeves, USA, ca.1965
(p.27)

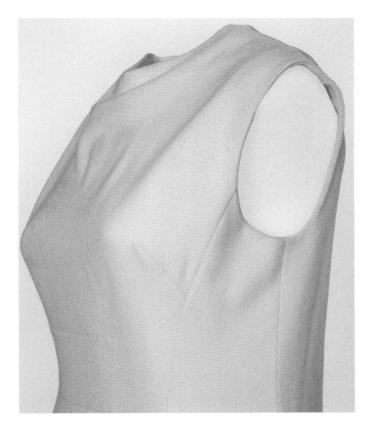

Black zibeline
sleeveless cocktail
dress, USA, ca.1965
(p.28)

Cream wool crepe
sheath dress with
matching coat,
trimmed in pink wool,
France, ca.1965
(p.28)

Pink, blue and yellow
wool tweed short-
sleeved sheath dress,
USA, ca.1966
(p.29)

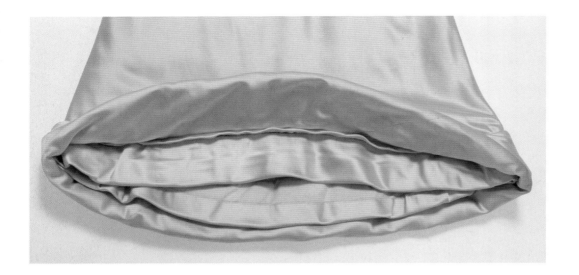

Cream silk satin sheath
dress with padded
hem, USA, ca.1966
(p.29)

Cream wool collarless
cropped jacket,
USA, ca.1967
(back view)
(p.30)

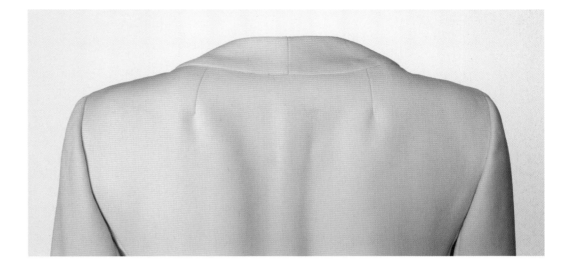

Black crepe sheath
dress, USA, ca.1967
(p.29)

Black silk faille
¾-length jacket,
USA, ca.1968
(p.31)

Greige wool crepe
sleeveless mini-
cocktail dress
with ruffle trim,
USA, ca.1968
(back view)
(p.30)

Ivory antique satin
floor-length A-line
dress, USA, ca.1969
(p.32)

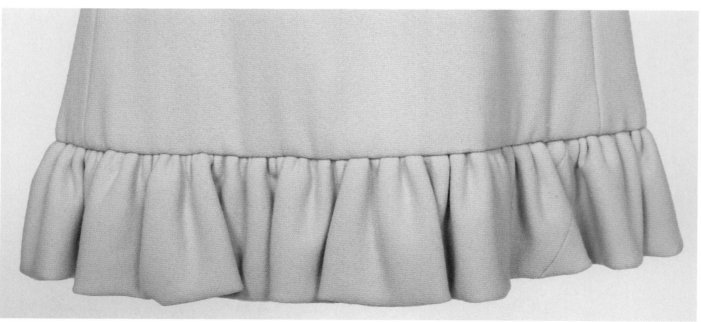

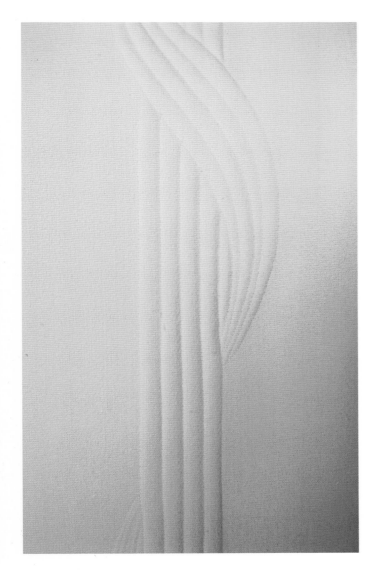

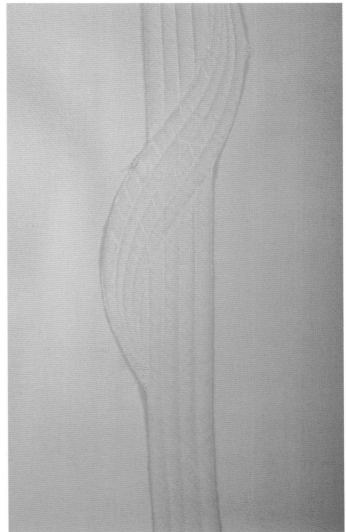

Yellow wool short-
sleeved sheath dress,
USA, ca.1969
(p.33)

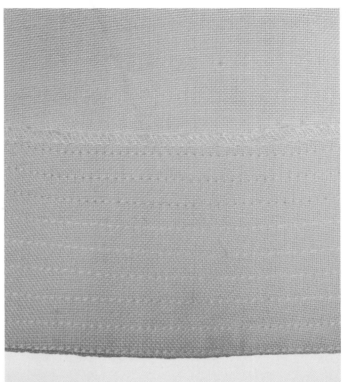

Turquoise wool double-breasted skirt suit, France, ca.1970 (p.33)

Purple and white checked wool long-sleeved dress with flared skirt, USA, ca.1970 (p.34)

Cream wool challis bodice with long sleeves and circular peplum, USA, ca.1985 (p.35)

Pleats, Frills & Flounces

Cream cotton
shirtwaist blouse with
low square neckline
and modified sailor
collar, USA, ca.1917
(p.10)

Ivory silk sleeveless
sheath dress with
lace flounced skirt,
USA, ca.1924
(p.12)

Robin's-egg-blue silk
taffeta sleeveless *robe
de style*, USA, ca.1924
(p.11)

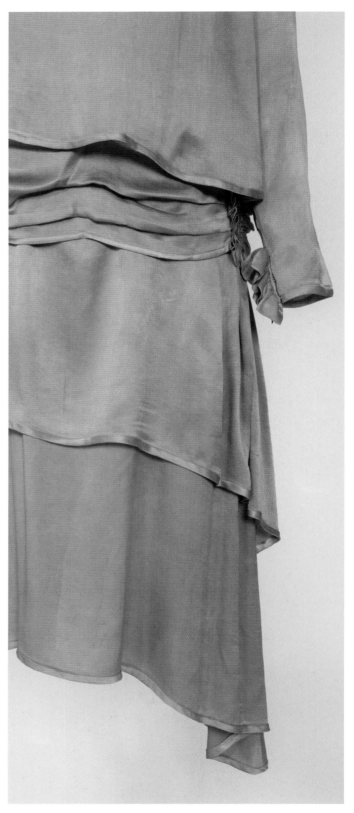

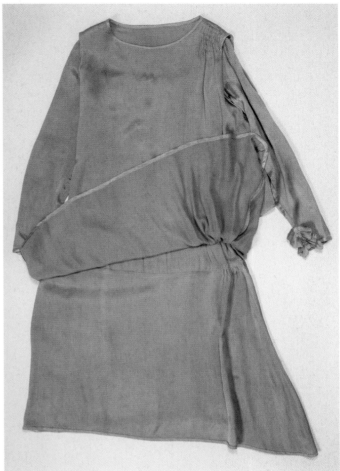

Black satin long-sleeved evening dress with cream lace sleeve and hem detailing, USA, ca.1927 (p.13)

Cream georgette dress and jacket, USA, ca.1927 (p.12)

Oyster-colored silk crepe long-sleeved asymmetrical day dress, USA, ca.1927 (p.13)

Black crepe evening
dress with taffeta
ruffles at collar,
hips, and cuffs,
England, ca.1928
(p.13)

Fuchsia silk georgette
day dress embellished
with horizontal, pleated
ruffles, USA, ca.1930
(p.14)

Black wool crepe day
dress with black devoré
sleeves and collar,
USA, ca.1932
(p.14)

Yellow and red printed
cotton bell-bottomed
pants, USA, ca.1932
(p.14)

Floral-print chiffon
dress with ruffles at
neckline and hem,
USA, ca.1935
(p.14)

Yellow, hot-pink and
gray printed short-
sleeved day dress,
USA, ca.1938
(back view)
(p.17)

PLEATS, FRILLS & FLOUNCES

277

Black synthetic crepe day dress with pleated front, USA, ca.1939 (p.18)

Black crepe short-sleeved dress with apron front and braid trim, USA, ca.1940 (back view) (p.19)

Mauve rayon crepe
cocktail dress with
embroidered front and
peplum, USA, ca.1942
(p.19)

Brown crepe floor-
length dress with front
swag and embroidered
neckline, USA, ca.1942
(p.19)

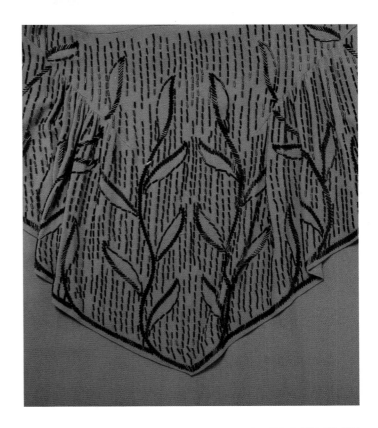

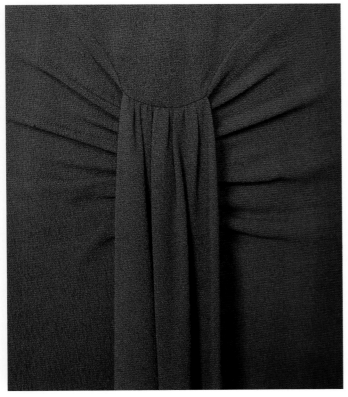

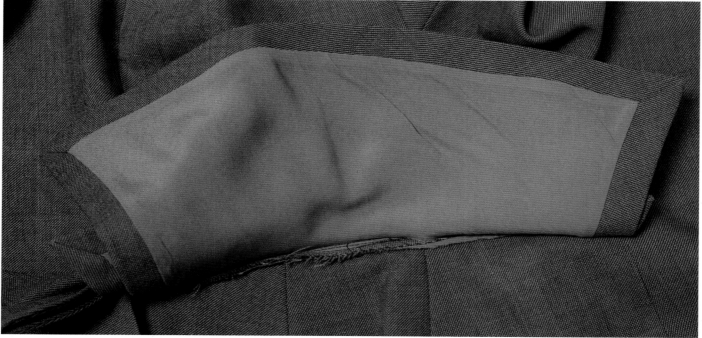

Brown skirt suit,
USA, ca.1949
(back view)
(p.21)

Sage-green printed
cotton full-skirted
dress, USA, ca.1950
(p.22)

Green and navy-
blue 'Black Watch'
plaid shirt-jacket,
USA, ca.1949
(back view)
(p.21)

Navy-blue silk
taffeta shirt dress,
USA, ca.1950
(p.22)

Yellow printed cotton
one-piece swimsuit,
USA, ca.1955
(p.24)

Orange and yellow
printed cotton one-
piece swimsuit, USA,
ca.1955
(p.24)

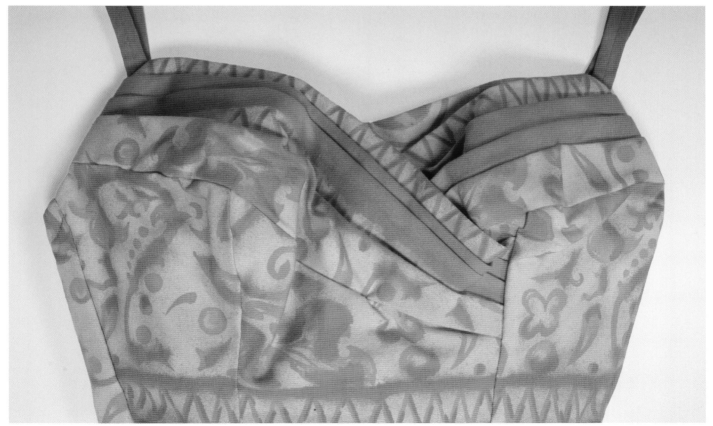

Brown crepe short-sleeved cocktail dress, USA, ca.1942 (p.20)

Black silk chiffon full-skirted cocktail dress, USA, ca.1958 (p.25)

Taupe silk cocktail
dress, USA, ca.1958
(p.25)

Green, red, yellow and
blue printed cotton
full-skirted dress,
USA, ca.1960
(p.26)

Blue and white striped
full-skirted day
dress with large bow,
USA, ca.1963
(p.27)

Black synthetic satin
sleeveless sheath
dress with scalloped,
pleated ruffle at hem,
USA, ca.1965
(p.28)

Yellow silk faille
evening dress,
USA, ca.1965
(back view)
(p.27)

Greige wool crepe
sleeveless mini-
cocktail dress
with ruffle trim,
USA, ca.1968
(p.30)

Gray wool long-sleeved
dress with pink velvet
bow and cream satin
collar and cuffs,
USA, ca.1968
(p.31)

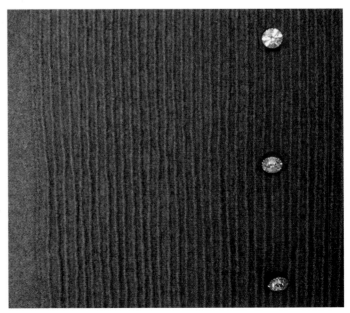

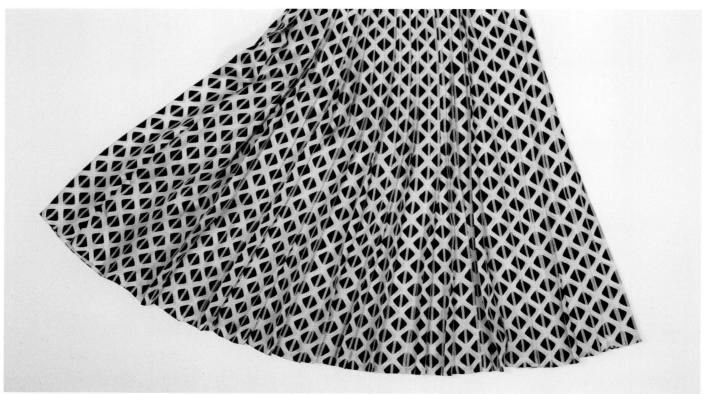

Green and beige
houndstooth-print
silk drop-waisted
dress with long sleeves
and jewel neckline,
USA, ca.1970
(p.33)

Black and yellow
printed skirt suit,
USA, ca.1970
(p.34)

Purple and white
checked wool long-
sleeved dress with
and flared skirt,
USA, ca.1970
(p.34)

PLEATS, FRILLS & FLOUNCES

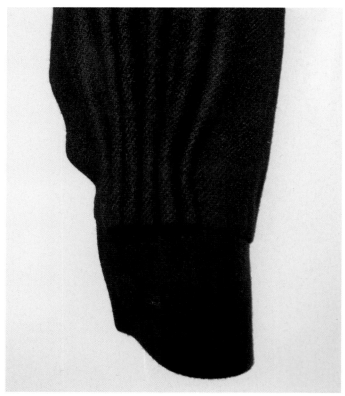

Cream wool challis
bodice with long
sleeves and circular
peplum, USA, ca.1985
(p.35)

Black wool waist-length
jacket, USA, ca.1994
(p.35)

Black silk satin ruffle-
pocket jacket, USA,
ca.1995
(p.35)

Embellishment

Hot-pink velveteen
jacket with soutache
trim and silk floss
embroidery, Italy,
ca.1913
(p.10)

White linen jacket with
inset striped vest, USA,
ca.1914 (back view)
(p.10)

Navy-blue cashmere
skirt suit with
embroidered peplum,
USA, ca.1916
(back view)
(p.10)

VINTAGE DETAILS

Purple silk corduroy
skirt suit, USA, ca.1917
(p.10)

Cream silk short-
sleeved day dress with
cream lace overskirt,
USA, ca.1920
(p.10)

Brown devoré evening
dress, USA, ca.1922
(p.11)

Brown silk georgette
day dress with
turquoise and brown
satin ribbon bows,
USA, ca.1922
(p.11)

Back view of left dress

Silver lace dress
over cream silk
taffeta underdress,
USA, ca.1923
(p.11)

Robin's-egg-blue silk
taffeta sleeveless *robe
de style*, USA, ca.1924
(p.11)

Black velvet *robe
de style* with jagged
hem and poppy trim,
USA, ca.1924
(p.11)

Ivory silk sleeveless
sheath dress with
lace flounced skirt,
USA, ca.1924
(p.12)

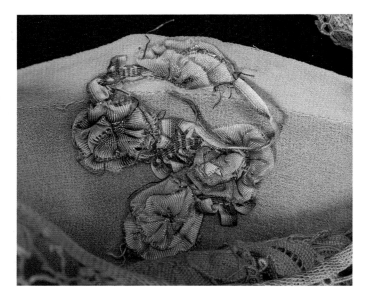

Black satin dress with handmade lace inset at front, USA, ca.1925 (p.12)

Rose-pink chiffon long-sleeved knee-length dress with cream lace inset at front, sleeves and hem, USA, ca.1925 (p.12)

VINTAGE DETAILS

Black satin coat
embellished with
cotton-floss cross
stitch in floral pattern,
USA, ca.1927
(p.13)

Cream georgette
dress and jacket,
USA, ca.1927
(p.12)

Oyster-colored silk
crepe long-sleeved
asymmetrical day
dress, USA, ca.1927
(p.13)

White silk taffeta and
silk net party dress,
USA, ca.1929
(p.13)

Floral-print chiffon
dress with ruffles
at neckline and hem,
USA, ca.1935
(p.14)

EMBELLISHMENT

309

Black synthetic crepe evening dress embellished with silk flowers and beaded wheat motif, USA, ca.1935 (p.15)

Black silk velvet and cream lace evening dress, USA, ca.1935 (p.15)

Purple velvet floor-
length evening dress,
USA, ca.1935
(p.15)

Green chenille knitted
dress with ¾-length
skirt and sleeves,
USA, ca.1935
(p.15)

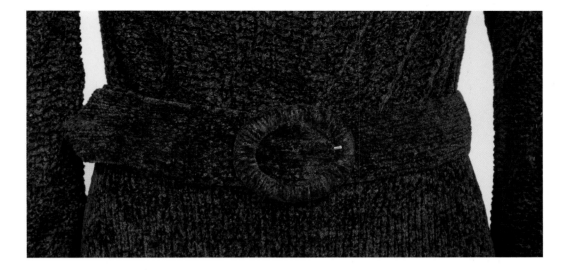

Pale peach silk
day dress with
bow detailing,
England, ca.1937
(p.17)

Black silk crepe day
dress with inset satin
bow detailing and
fagotting, USA, ca.1938
(p.17)

Burgundy velvet
cocktail dress with
beaded bow trim,
USA, ca.1939
(p.17)

Black crepe short-sleeved dress with apron front and braid trim, USA, ca.1940 (p.19)

Black silk single-sleeved fringed wrap, USA, ca.1940 (p.19)

Brown crepe floor-length dress with front swag and embroidered neckline, USA, ca.1942 (p.19)

Mauve rayon crepe
cocktail dress with
embroidered front and
peplum, USA, ca.1942
(p.19)

Black crepe long-
sleeved dress with
fringe peplum,
USA, ca.1942
(p.20)

Brown crepe short-
sleeved cocktail dress,
USA, ca.1942
(p.20)

Black crepe suit with
white 'doily' trim, USA,
ca.1943
(p.20)

Navy-blue wool blazer
with engineered stripe
detailing, USA, ca.1946
(back view)
(p.21)

Brown skirt suit,
USA, ca.1949
(back view)
(p.21)

Red wool felt circle
skirt with black braid
and embroidery
decoration, USA,
ca.1950
(p.22)

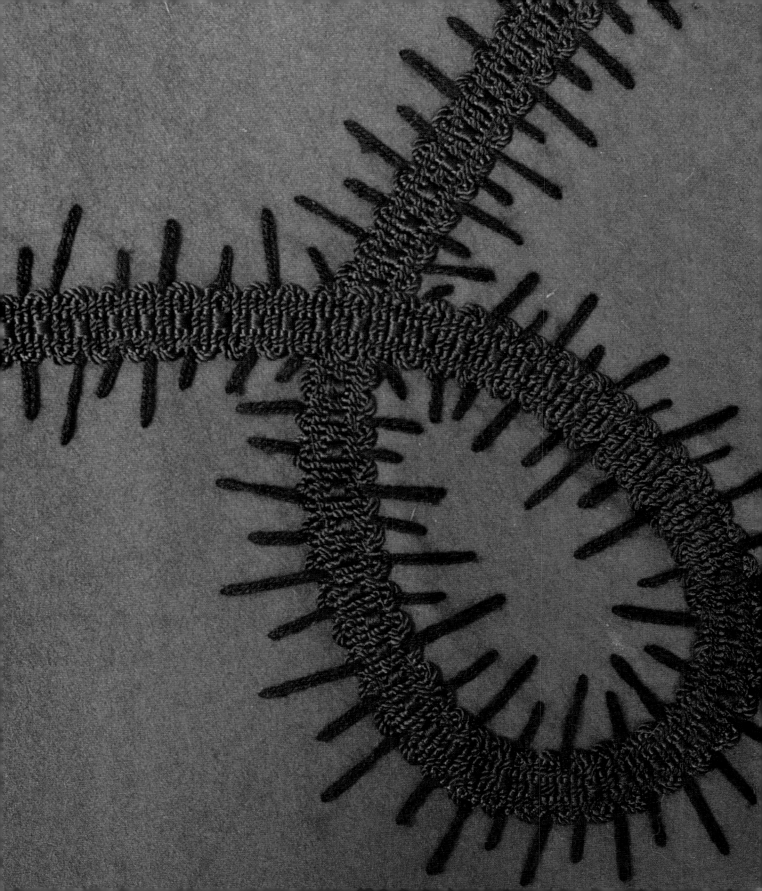

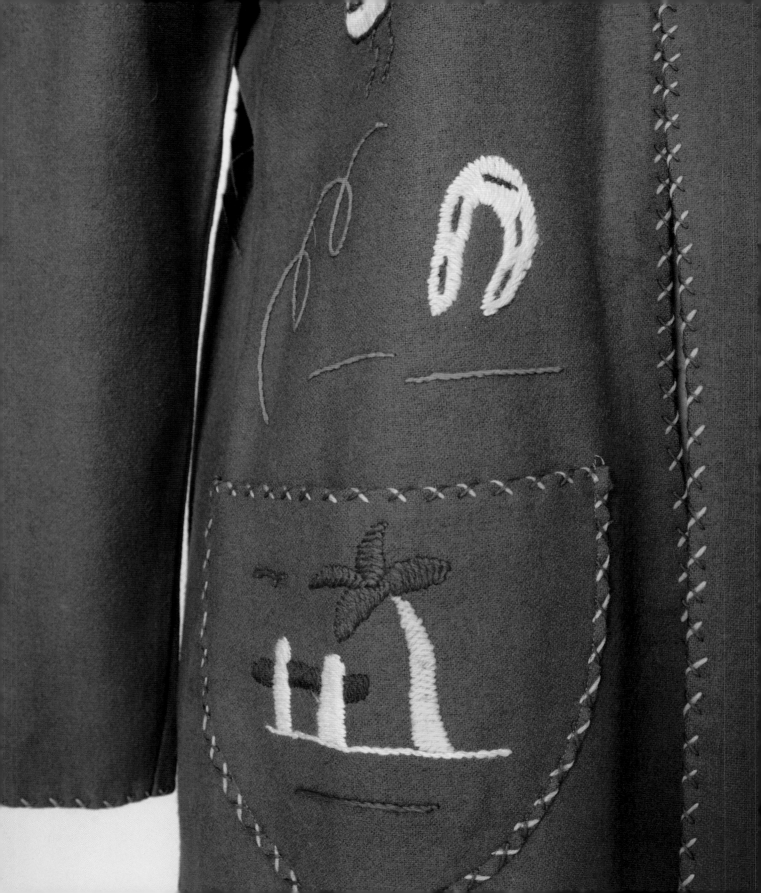

Overleaf

Turquoise jacket
embroidered with
toreador motifs,
Mexico, ca.1952
(p.23)

Back view of left jacket

Cream satin ¾-length
sleeve cocktail dress
brocaded with green
and pink motifs, and
green bow at bust,
USA, ca.1956
(p.22)

Black silk chiffon
cocktail dress
with floral hemline
detailing, USA, ca.1958
(p.25)

Turquoise silk satin
two-piece sheath
evening dress,
USA, ca.1960
(p.25)

Back view of left dress

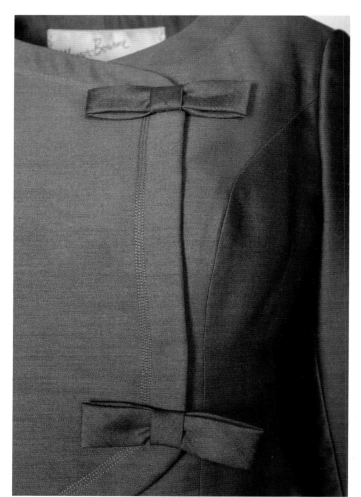

VINTAGE DETAILS

Red silk shantung
dress with matching
bolero, USA, ca.1960
(dress only)
(p.26)

Bronze-colored
shantung skirt suit
with ¾-length sleeves,
USA, ca.1962
(p.26)

Green, white and blue
sprig-print cotton day
dress, USA, ca.1963
(p.27)

Blue and white striped
full-skirted day
dress with large bow,
USA, ca.1963
(p.27)

Gray wool sheath dress embroidered with pussy willow, USA, ca.1963 (p.27)

Pink and white patterned scoop-necked dress with matching short jacket, USA, ca.1965 (dress only) (p.27)

Apple-green and gold brocade mini-cocktail dress, USA, ca.1965 (p.28)

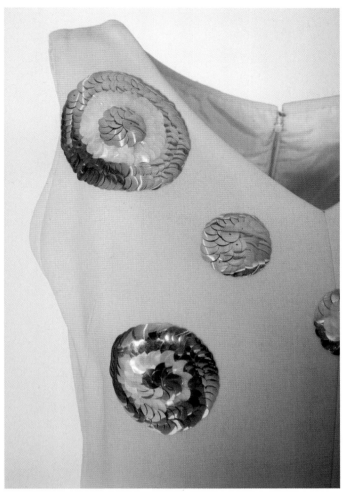

Yellow silk faille
evening dress,
USA, ca.1965
(p.27)

Brown crepe long-
sleeved tunic with
sequined bands on
center front and cuffs,
France, ca.1966
(p.29)

Cream wool sheath
dress embellished with
silver-sequin polka-
dots, France, ca.1966
(p.29)

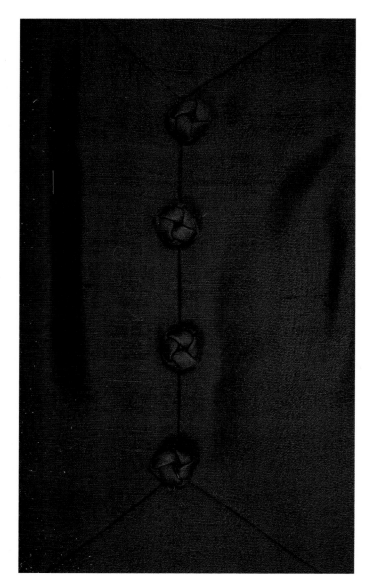

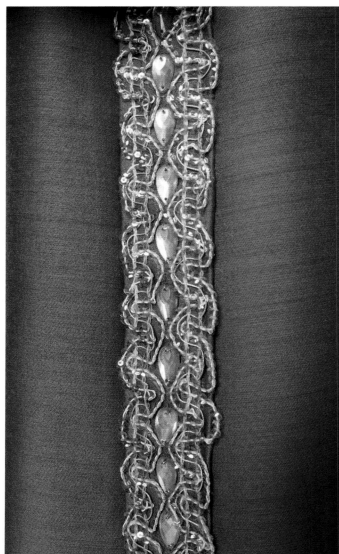

Black crepe sheath
dress, USA, ca.1967
(p.29)

Bottle-green zibeline
cocktail dress,
USA, ca.1967
(p.29)

Greige wool crepe
sleeveless mini-
cocktail dress
with ruffle trim,
USA, ca.1968
(p.30)

Cream silk tunic with
beaded bib and cuffs,
USA, ca.1968
(p.31)

Ivory antique satin floor-length A-line dress, USA, ca.1969 (p.32)

Navy-blue and cream wool double-knit short-sleeved sheath dress, Italy, ca.1969 (p.32)

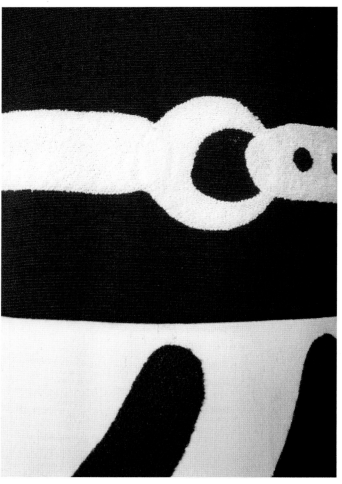

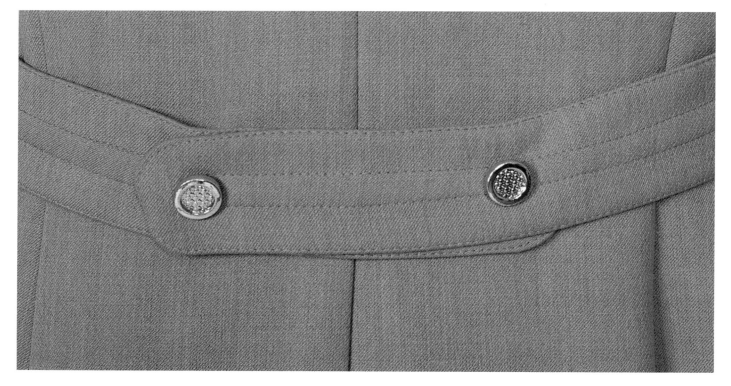

White seersucker
long-sleeved
minidress,
USA, ca.1969
(p.32)

White and black
silk dress trimmed
with silver studs,
USA, ca.1969
(p.33)

Taupe sleeveless
sheath dress with
matching long-sleeved
coat, USA, ca.1969
(back view)
(p.32)

Turquoise wool double-
breasted skirt suit,
France, ca.1970
(back view)
(p.33)

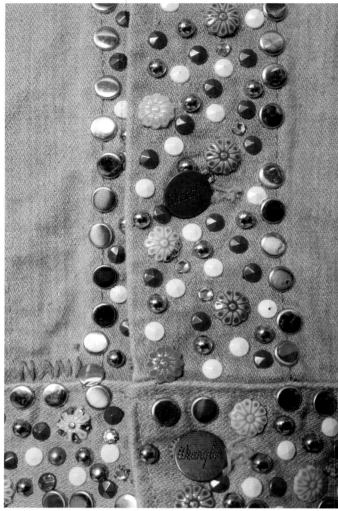

Denim jacket
embellished with
studs and rhinestones,
USA, ca.1970
(p.33)

Back view of left jacket

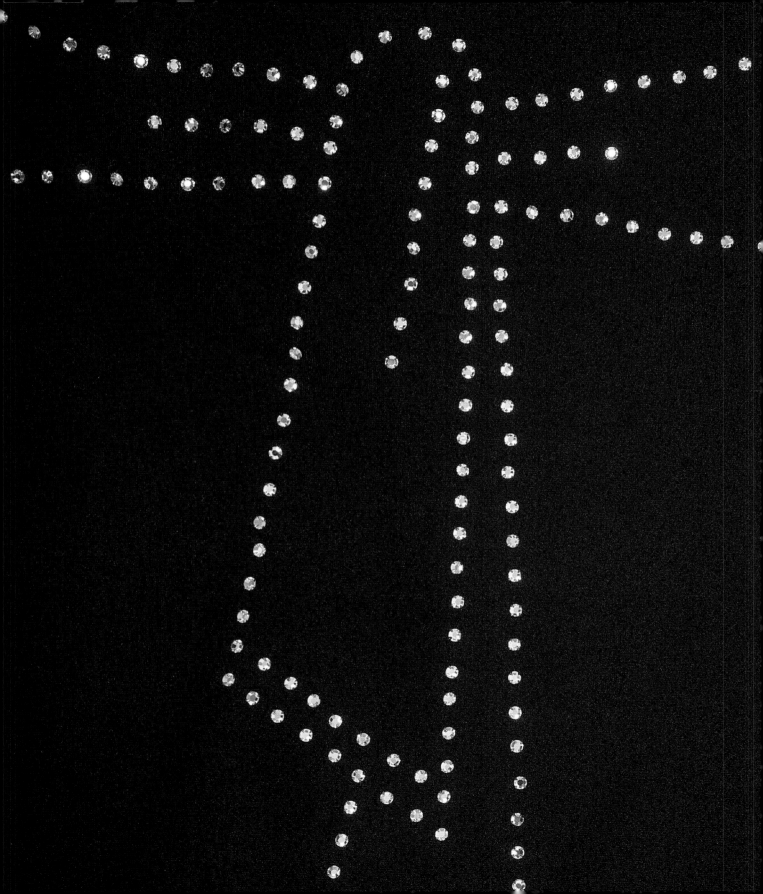

Black polyester crepe dress with lace sleeves and rhinestone trompe l'oeil belt, USA, ca.1975 (p.34)

Cream wool challis bodice with long sleeves and circular peplum, USA, ca.1985 (p.35)

Surface

Cream silk short-sleeved day dress with cream lace overskirt, USA, ca.1920 (p.10)

Brown devoré evening dress, USA, ca.1922 (p.11)

Silver lace dress
over cream silk
taffeta underdress,
USA, ca.1923
(p.11)

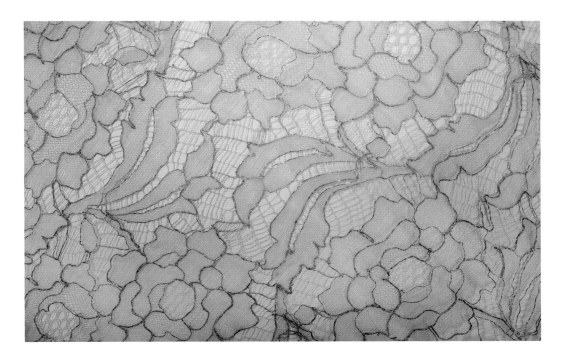

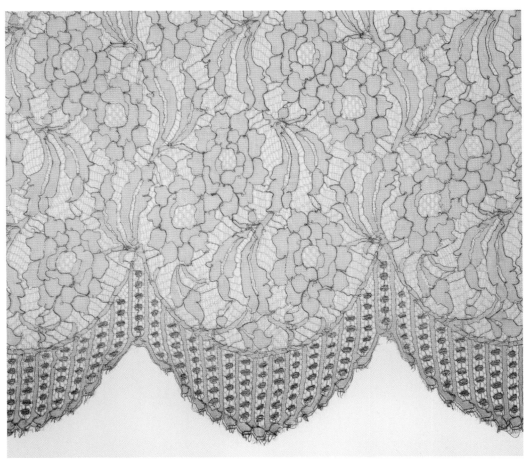

Rose-pink chiffon long-sleeved knee-length dress with cream lace inset at front, sleeves and hem, USA, ca.1925 (p.12)

Purple devoré coat,
USA, ca.1926
(p.12)

Natural linen
sheath dress and
jacket printed with
Art Deco motifs,
England, ca.1927
(p.13)

Back view of left dress
and jacket

Blue, yellow and red
paisley-print cotton
voile day dress with
drawstring pockets,
USA, ca.1932
(p.14)

Red and pink printed
cotton day dress,
USA, ca.1935
(p.16)

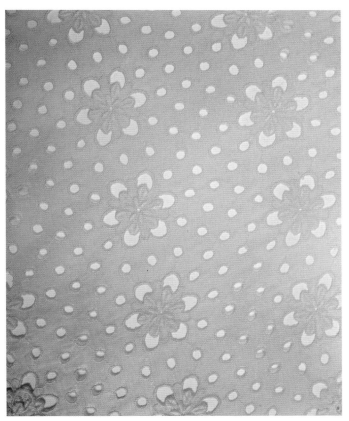

White, green, yellow,
red and violet bamboo-
print silk crepe evening
dress, USA, ca.1935
(p.16)

Floral-print chiffon
dress with ruffles at
neckline and hem,
USA, ca.1935
(p.14)

White cotton eyelet-
embroidered dress
with cape collar,
USA, ca.1935
(p.15)

Green chenille knitted
dress with ¾-length
skirt and sleeves,
USA, ca.1935
(p.15)

Yellow, hot-pink and
gray printed short-
sleeved day dress,
USA, ca.1938
(p.17)

Blue synthetic crepe day dress with cream and blue lace yoke and sleeves, USA, ca.1939 (p.18)

Multicolored hand-marbled silk crepe day dress, England, ca.1939 (p.18)

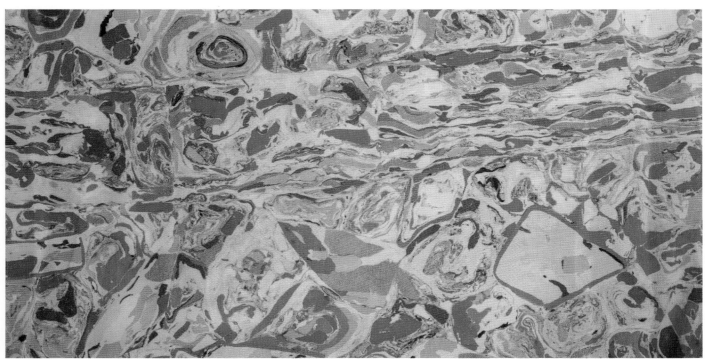

Gray and black printed
nylon day dress,
USA, ca.1939
(p.18)

Red wool tweed blazer,
USA, ca.1944
(p.20)

Black and brown
wool tweed jacket
with princess-seam
detailing, USA, ca.1952
(p.23)

Yellow printed cotton
one-piece swimsuit,
USA, ca.1955
(p.24)

Brown and black
diagonal-striped wool
coat, USA, ca.1955
(p.24)

Cream satin ¾-length
sleeve cocktail dress
brocaded with green
and pink motifs, and
green bow at bust,
USA, ca.1956
(p.24)

Green, red, yellow and
blue printed cotton
full-skirted dress,
USA, ca.1960
(p.26)

Gray wool sheath
dress embroidered
with pussy willow,
USA, ca.1963
(p.27)

Red and cream
printed silk twill
long-sleeved dress
with mock turtleneck,
USA, ca.1967
(p.30)

Yellow satin long-
sleeved blouse with
patchwork floor-length
skirt, USA, ca.1967
(p.30)

Orange Art-Deco-
print chiffon long-
sleeved sheath dress,
USA, ca.1968
(p.31)

Black, red, pink, blue
and yellow wool long-
sleeved ankle-length
turtleneck dress with
embroidered detailing,
USA, ca.1969
(p.32)

Black velvet jumpsuit
with appliquéd
organdie sleeves and
hem, USA, ca.1969
(p.32)

Gray wool long-sleeved
dress with pink velvet
bow and cream satin
collar and cuffs,
USA, ca.1968
(p.31)

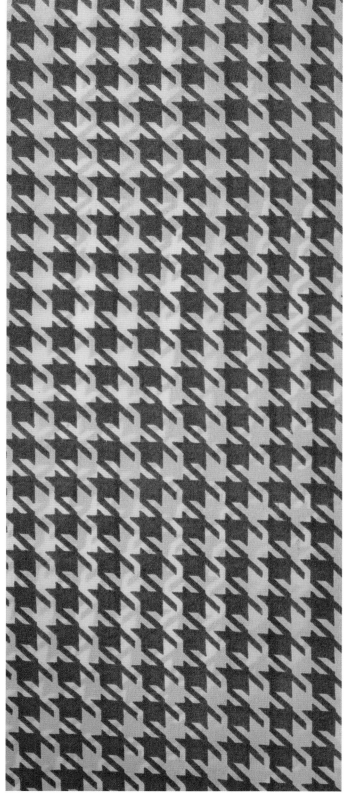

White seersucker long-
sleeved minidress,
USA, ca.1969
(p.32)

Green and beige
houndstooth-print
silk drop-waisted
dress with long sleeves
and jewel neckline,
USA, ca.1970
(p.33)

Black and yellow print
skirt suit, USA, ca.1970
(p.34)

Cream and eggplant-
colored triangle-
print tunic and skirt
ensemble, USA, ca.1970
(p.33)

Construction

Navy-blue cashmere
skirt suit with
embroidered peplum,
USA, ca.1916
(p.10)

Robin's-egg-blue silk
taffeta sleeveless *robe
de style*, USA, ca.1924
(p.11)

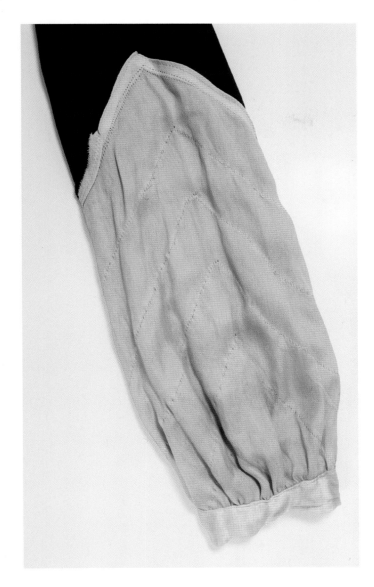

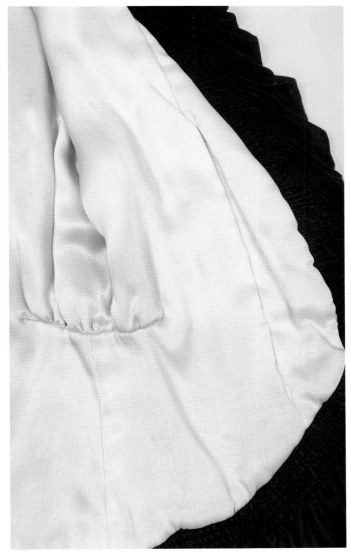

Black velvet *robe de style* with jagged hem and poppy trim, USA, ca.1924 (p.11)

Black satin long-sleeved evening dress with cream lace sleeve and hem detailing, USA, ca.1927 (p.13)

Black velvet evening coat trimmed with padded collar and ruffle detailing, USA, ca.1935 (p.16)

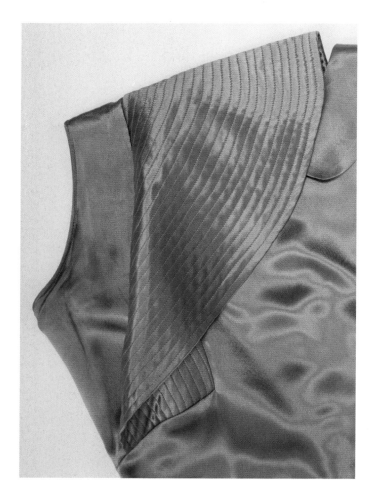

Spring green bias-cut
satin evening dress,
USA, ca.1935
(p.16)

Burgundy velvet
cocktail dress with
short ruched sleeves,
USA, ca.1938
(p.17)

Burgundy velvet
cocktail dress with
beaded bow trim,
USA, ca.1939
(p.17)

Black synthetic crepe day dress with pleated front, USA, ca.1939 (p.18)

Brown crepe floor-length dress with front swag and embroidered neckline, USA, ca.1942 (p.19)

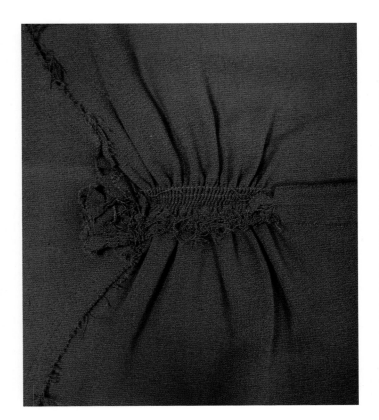

CONSTRUCTION

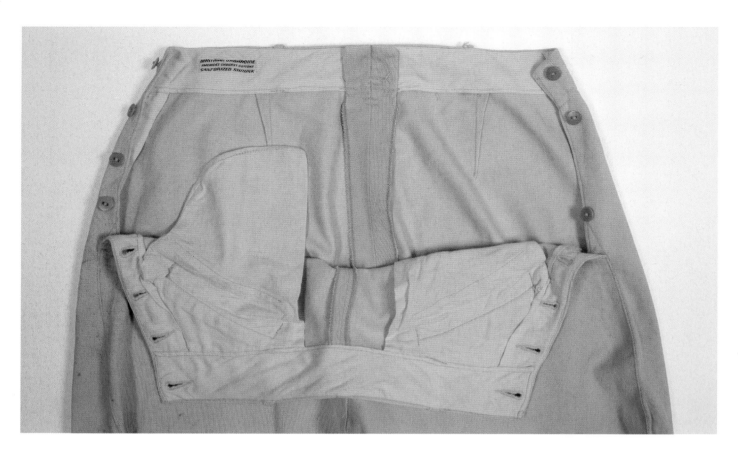

Orange and brown
plaid wool outerwear
jacket with cream wool
gabardine jodhpurs,
USA, ca.1940
(p.19)

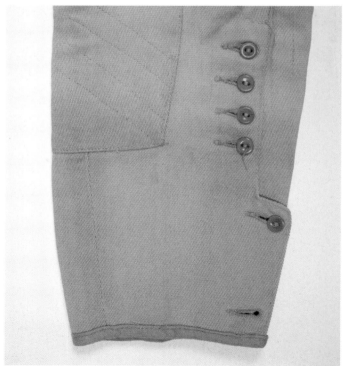

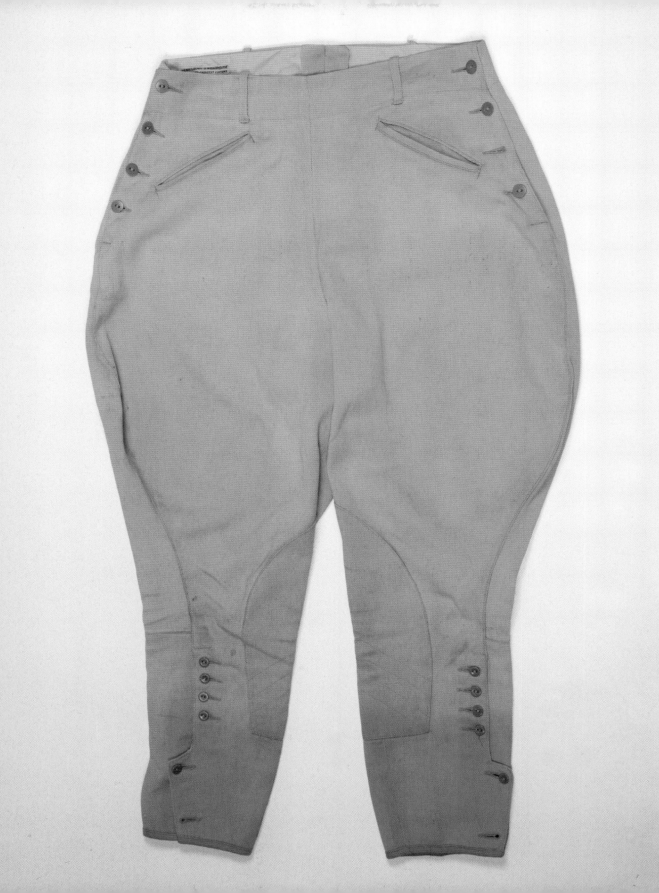

Gray-blue wool crepe day dress with fringe-trimmed bound pockets, USA, ca.1945 (p.20)

Brown wool skirt suit, USA, ca.1947 (p.21)

Navy-blue silk
taffeta shirt dress,
USA, ca.1950
(p.22)

Gray wool skirt suit,
USA, ca.1950
(p.22)

Olive-green wool
double-knit day dress,
USA, ca.1951
(p.23)

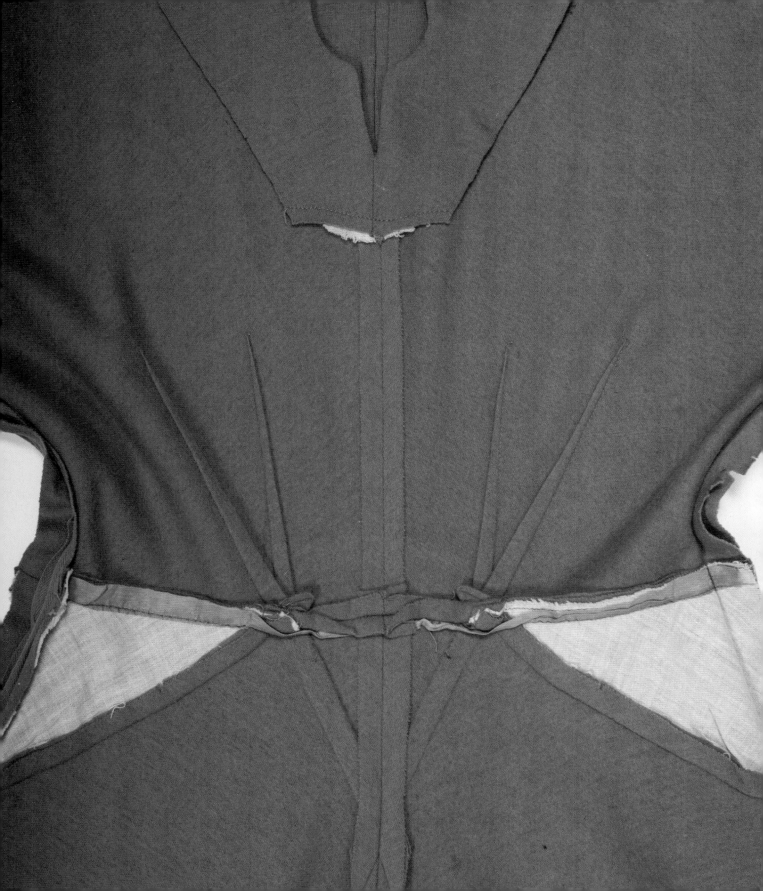

Yellow printed cotton
one-piece swimsuit,
USA, ca.1955
(p.24)

Back view of left
swimsuit

VINTAGE DETAILS

Orange and yellow
printed cotton
one-piece swimsuit,
USA, ca.1955
(p.24)

Back view of left
swimsuit

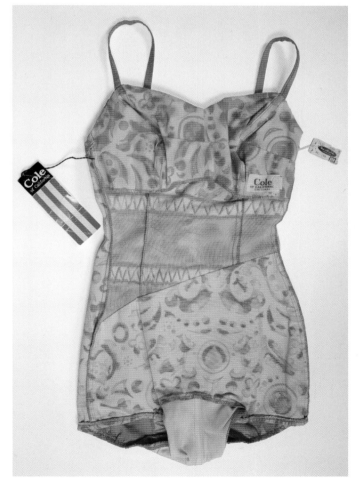

Taupe silk cocktail
dress, USA, ca.1958
(p.25)

Turquoise silk satin
two-piece sheath
evening dress,
USA, ca.1960
(p.25)

Bodice of left dress

Yellow silk faille
evening dress,
USA, ca.1965
(p.27)

Black zibeline
sleeveless cocktail
dress, USA, ca.1965
(p.28)

Bronze-colored
sleeveless cocktail
dress with
patch pockets,
Denmark, ca.1965
(p.28)

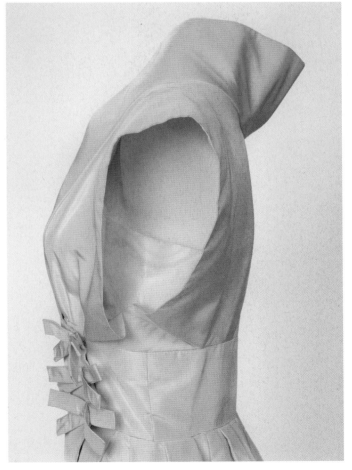

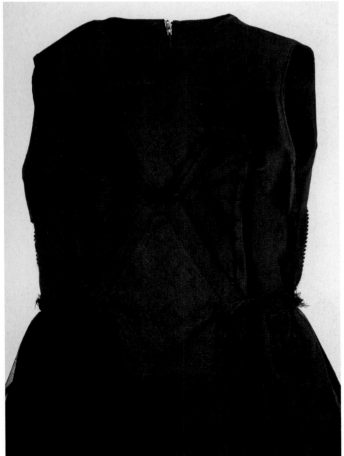

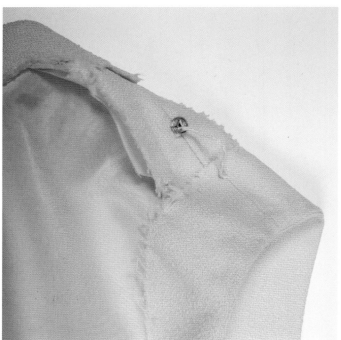

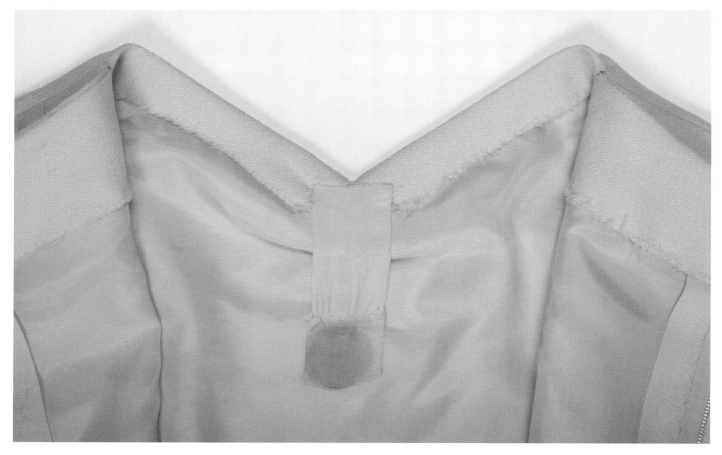

Oatmeal-colored wool
evening dress and
matching jacket with
hot-pink rhinestone
buttons, USA, ca.1965
(dress only)
(p.28)

Cream wool sheath
dress embellished with
silver-sequin polka-
dots, France, ca.1966
(p.29)

Cream wool crepe
sheath dress with
matching coat,
trimmed in pink wool,
France, ca.1965
(dress only)
(p.28)

Pink, blue and yellow
wool tweed short-
sleeved sheath dress,
USA, ca.1966
(p.29)

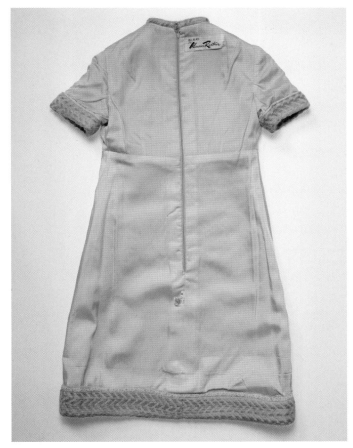

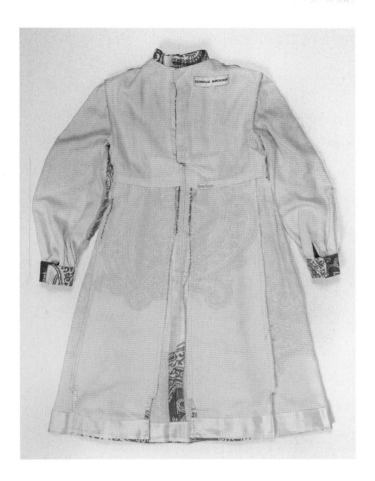

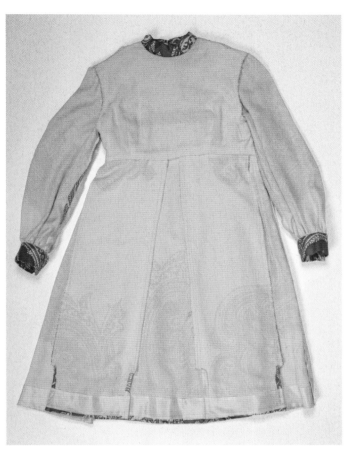

Black crepe sheath
dress, USA, ca.1967
(p.29)

Yellow satin long-
sleeved blouse with
patchwork floor-length
skirt, USA, ca.1967
(p.30)

Red and cream
printed silk twill
long-sleeved dress
with mock turtleneck,
USA, ca.1967
(p.30)

Gray wool long-sleeved
dress with pink velvet
bow and cream satin
collar and cuffs,
USA, ca.1968
(p.31)

Greige wool crepe
sleeveless mini cocktail
dress with ruffle trim,
USA, ca.1968
(p.30)

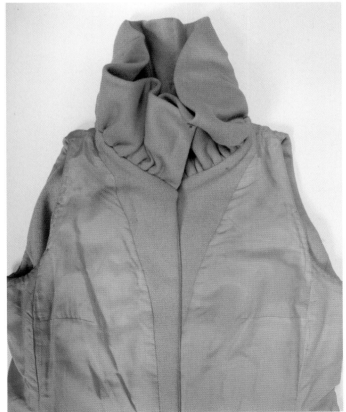

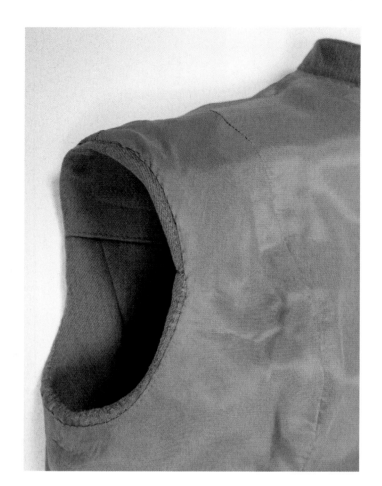

VINTAGE DETAILS

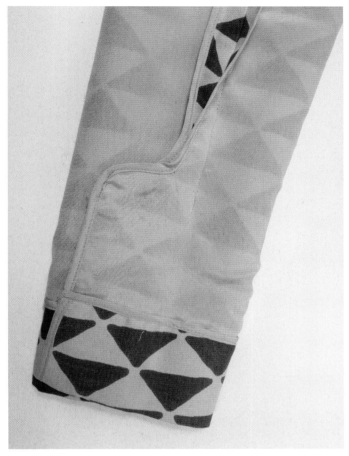

Taupe sleeveless
sheath dress with
matching long-sleeved
coat, USA, ca.1969
(p.32)

White and black
silk dress trimmed
with silver studs,
USA, ca.1969
(p.33)

Cream and eggplant-
colored triangle-
print tunic and skirt
ensemble, USA, ca.1970
(p.33)

VINTAGE DETAILS

Green and beige
houndstooth-print silk
drop-waisted dress,
USA, ca.1970
(p.33)

Black and yellow
printed skirt suit,
USA, ca.1970
(p.34)

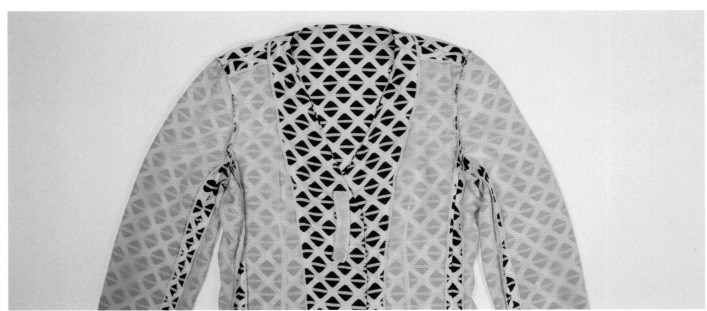

Cream wool challis
bodice with long
sleeves and circular
peplum, USA, ca.1985
(back view)
(p.35)

Black silk satin jacket
with clover-leaf
neckline, USA, ca.1995
(p.35)

Credits & Acknowledgments

Credits

All photography by Stephen Sartori © Syracuse University, the Sue Ann Genet Costume Collection.

The following garments featured in the Visual Index appear in the private collection of Basia Szkutnicka: p.11TL, p.13TR, p.13MR, p.13BL, p.14TL, p.16ML, p.17TL, p.17MR, p.18TR, p.18MR, p.27BL, p.28BL, p.34BL. All other garments are from the Sue Ann Genet Costume Collection.

Acknowledgments

Ann Clarke, Dean College of Visual and Performing Arts, Syracuse University

Dr. James Fathers, Director School of Design, VPA, SU

Todd Conover, Coordinator Fashion Design Program, VPA, SU

Lauren Tagliaferro, Registrar Sue Ann Genet Costume Collection

Suzanne Bartlett, Administrative Specialist

Christopher Cederquist

Audrey Grant

Amy de la Haye

Jean Henry

Sarah Elmer Howard

Erica Jensen

Peter Mars

Carolyn and Ellsworth Mayer

Susan Mayer

Thanks to commissioning editor Sophie Drysdale for championing this project, to Melissa Danny for her tireless editing of the book, and to Mark Fairman, Hamzi Hamdan, Chris Ennis and Imad Douglas at DL Imaging Ltd, London.

Special acknowledgment to the family of Sue and Leon Genet for their continued support of the Sue Ann Genet Costume Collection:

Pam Genet Barsh

Wendy Genet Kaplan

Jill Genet Waller

Particular thanks to the following donors:

Marolyn Caldwell

Nancy Stokes Milnes

Susan Mack Saril